PSYCHOANALYSIS

AND

RELIGION

ERICH FROMM

NEW HAVEN & LONDON · YALE UNIVERSITY PRESS

D1052453

Distributed in Great Britain, Europe, and
Africa by Yale University Press, Ltd., London;
in Canada by McGill-Queen's University Press,
Montreal; in Mexico by Centro Interamericano de
Libros Académicos, Mexico City; in Australasia
by Australia and New Zealand Book Co., Pty.,
Ltd., Artarmon, New South Wales; in India by
UBS Publishers' Distributors Pvt., Ltd., Delhi;
in Japan by John Weatherhill, Inc., Tokyo.

FOREWORD

THIS BOOK can be considered as a continuation of thoughts expressed in *Man for Himself*, an inquiry into the psychology of ethics. Ethics and religion are closely interrelated and therefore there is some overlapping. But I have tried in this book to focus on the problem of religion while in *Man for Himself* the emphasis is entirely on ethics.

The views expressed in these chapters are in no sense representative of "psychoanalysis." There are psychoanalysts who are practicing religionists as well as others who consider the interest in religion a symptom of unsolved emotional conflicts. The position taken in this book differs from both and is, at most, representative of the thinking of a third group of psychoanalysts.

I wish to express my gratitude to my wife not only for the many suggestions which have been directly incorporated into these chapters but, far beyond this, for what I owe to her searching and penetrating mind which has so greatly contributed to my own development and hence indirectly to my ideas about religion.

E. F.

FOREWORD II

WHEN ONE writes a new foreword to a book that was published sixteen years ago, the first question the author asks himself is whether he will want to correct the text in any essential points that he now considers to be erroneous. Since, during these years, my ideas have been constantly changing and, as I hope, developing, I was quite prepared in rereading the book to find a number of statements I might like to change. To my surprise I found that I felt no need for changes in essential points and have no objection to having the book reprinted again as it stands.

The next question an author would ask himself is whether he should expand on what he wrote many years earlier. The answer to this question is definitely in the affirmative. I stressed in the text the importance of differentiating between the religious thought concept and the human experience behind it. But I did not go far enough in describing what it is that could be called "religious experience," regardless of what the thought concept may be. If I were to write the book today I would expand the chapter on "Some Types of Religious Experience." This is not the place to do so, but there is one point I want to mention: for the religious person, whether he is a "believer" or not, life is a problem; the fact of having been born raises a question that man must answer. The most important task of his life, then, is to find an answer to this question; not an answer in thought only, but an answer in his whole being, in his way of living. For this person life is not something "given" which requires no other meaning than to eat and drink, survive, have pleasure, and take part in events in accordance to one's ethical norms. He senses the profound existential dichotomies that beset life: that between being free—yet determined; separate — yet united; filled with knowledge—yet profoundly ignorant. He suffers from his feeling of separateness. His activity is directed toward finding the optimal solution to these contradictions, while at the same time he knows that there is no solution; and there is no goal in life that is not subordinated to this attempt. Here lies, in fact, the difference between the hedonistic and the ethical man on the one hand, and the "religious" man on the other.

Rather than to yield to the temptation to continue to present thoughts about the nature of religious experience which, even if correct, must necessarily be insufficient in this context, I would point to a phenomenon which seems to make this problem particularly relevant in our time. The phenomenon I refer to is the humanist renaissance that is taking place within the Roman Catholic and the Protestant churches. This movement, greatly stimulated by Pope John XXIII, has led to a new dialogue, not only between Catholics and Protestants but also between theistic and nontheistic humanists. This dialogue does not proceed on the basis that its participants should relinquish their respective theistic or nontheistic thought concepts. But it implies that those involved in the dialogue must recognize that, beyond what man consciously thinks, there exists another dimension—that of what he feels. This inner experience is hardly expressible in words, yet those who share the experience know that what they have in common is more than that which divides them because of differences in thought concepts.

The names of Teilhard de Chardin, Hans Küng, and Karl Rahner are only a few of those who are representative of this developing humanism. The same development has occurred within Protestantism in an even more radical form. The position I refer to has become well known in recent years under the concept of "Godless Christianity." Dietrich Bonnhoefer, Karl Bultmann, and, in a less radical sense, Paul Tillich are representative names for this Protestant radical humanism.

Perhaps nothing could express the spirit of this type of humanism better than a sentence by Abbé Pire: "What matters is not the difference between believers and unbelievers, but between those who care and those who do not care."

Mexico City
March 1967   Erich Fromm

CONTENTS

I

THE PROBLEM

NEVER before has man come so close to the fulfillment of his most cherished hopes as today. Our scientific discoveries and technical achievements enable us to visualize the day when the table will be set for all who want to eat, a day when the human race will form a unified community and no longer live as separate entities. Thousands of years were needed for this unfolding of man's intellectual capacities, of his growing ability to organize society and to concentrate his energies purposefully. Man has created a new world with its own laws and destiny. Looking at his creation, he can say, truly, it is good.

But looking at himself what can he say? Has he come closer to the realization of another dream of mankind, that of the perfection of *man?* Of man loving his neighbor, doing justice, speaking truth, and realizing that which he potentially is, an image of God?

Raising the question is embarrassing since the answer is so painfully clear. While we have created wonderful things we have failed to make of ourselves beings for whom this tremendous effort would seem worthwhile. Ours is a life not of brotherliness, happiness, contentment but of spiritual chaos and bewilderment dangerously close to a state of madness—not the hysterical kind of madness which existed in the

Middle Ages but a madness akin to schizophrenia in which the contact with inner reality is lost and thought is split from affect.

Let us consider only some of the news items which we read every morning and evening. As a reaction to the water shortage in New York prayers for rain are suggested in churches and simultaneously rainmakers attempt to produce rain by chemical means. For over a year flying saucers have been reported; some say they do not exist, others that they are real and a new part of our own or a foreign power's military equipment, while others quite seriously claim that they are machines sent from the inhabitants of another planet. We are told that never has America had such a bright future as in this mid portion of the twentieth century, while on the same page the probability of a war is discussed and scientists argue whether the atomic weapon will or will not lead to the destruction of the globe.

People go to churches and listen to sermons in which the principles of love and charity are preached, and the very same people would consider themselves fools or worse if they hesitated to sell a commodity which they knew the customer could not afford. Children in Sunday school learn that honesty and integrity and concern for the soul should be the guiding principles of life, while "life" teaches us that to follow these principles makes us at best unrealistic dreamers. We have the most extraordinary possibilities for communication in print, radio, and television, and we are fed daily with nonsense which would be offensive to the intelligence of children were they not suckled on it. It is proclaimed by many voices that our way of life makes us happy. But how many people of these times are happy? It is interesting to remember a casual shot in *Life* magazine some time ago of a group of people waiting on a street corner for the green light. What was so remarkable and so shocking about this picture was that these people who all looked stunned and frightened had not witnessed a dreadful accident but, as the text had to explain, were merely average citizens going about their business.

We cling to the belief that we are happy; we teach our children that we are more advanced than any generation before us, that eventually no wish will remain unfulfilled and nothing will be out of our reach. The appearances support this belief, which is drummed into us endlessly.

But will our children hear a voice telling them where to go and what to live for? Somehow they feel, as all human beings do, that life must have a meaning—but what is it? Do they find it in the contradictions, double talk, and cynical resignation they encounter at every turn? They long for happiness, for truth, for justice, for love, for an object of devotion; are we able to satisfy their longing?

We are as helpless as they are. We do not know the answer because we even have forgotten to ask the question. We pretend that our life is based upon a solid foundation and ignore the shadows of uneasiness, anxiety, and confusion which never leave us.

To some people return to religion is the answer, not as an act of faith but in order to escape an intolerable doubt; they make this decision not out of devotion but in search of security. The student of the contemporary scene who is not concerned with the church but with man's *soul* considers this step another symptom of the failure of nerve.

Those who try to find a solution by returning to traditional religion are influenced by a view which is often proposed by religionists, that we have to choose between religion and a way of life which is concerned only with the satisfaction of our instinctual needs and material comfort; that if we do not believe in God we have no reason—and no right—to believe in the soul and its demands. Priests and ministers appear to be the only professional groups concerned with the soul, the only spokesmen for the ideals of love, truth, and justice.

Historically this was not always so. While in some cultures like that of Egypt the priests were the "physicians of the soul," in others such as Greece this function was at least partly assumed by philosophers. Socrates, Plato, Aristotle did not claim to speak in the name of any revelation but with the authority of reason and of their concern with man's happiness and the unfolding of his soul. They were concerned with man as an end in himself as the most significant subject matter of inquiry. Their treatises on philosophy and ethics were at the same time works on psychology. This tradition of antiquity was continued in the Renaissance and it is very characteristic that the first book which uses the word "Psychologia" in its title has the subtitle *Hoc est de Perfectione Hominis* (This is of the Perfection of Man).[1] It was during the Enlightenment that this tradition reached its highest point. Out of their belief in man's reason the philosophers of the Enlightenment, who were at the same time students of man's soul, affirmed man's independence from political shackles as well as from those of superstition and ignorance. They taught him to abolish those conditions of existence which required the maintenance of illusions. Their psychological inquiry was rooted in the attempt to discover the conditions for human happiness. Happiness, they said, can be achieved only when man has achieved inner freedom; only then can he be mentally healthy. But in the last few generations the rationalism of the Enlightenment has undergone drastic change. Drunk with a new material prosperity and success in mastering nature, man no longer has considered himself the primary concern of life and of theoretical inquiry. Reason as the means for discovering the truth and penetrating the surface to the essence of phenomena has been relinquished for intellect as a mere instrument to manipulate things and men. Man has ceased to believe that the power of reason can establish the validity of norms and ideas for human conduct.

This change in the intellectual and emotional climate has had a profound impact on the development of psychology as a science. Notwithstanding exceptional figures like Nietzsche and Kierkegaard, the

1. Rudolf Goeckel, 1590.

tradition in which psychology was a study of the soul concerned with man's virtue and happiness was abandoned. Academic psychology, trying to imitate the natural sciences and laboratory methods of weighing and counting, dealt with everything except the soul. It tried to understand those aspects of man which can be examined in the laboratory and claimed that conscience, value judgments, the knowledge of good and evil are metaphysical concepts, outside the problems of psychology; it was more often concerned with insignificant problems which fitted an alleged scientific method than with devising new methods to study the significant problems of man. Psychology thus became a science lacking its main subject matter, the soul; it was concerned with mechanisms, reaction formations, instincts, but not with the most specifically human phenomena: love, reason, conscience, values. Because the word *soul* has associations which include these higher human powers I use it here and throughout these chapters rather than the words "psyche" or "mind."

Then came Freud, the last great representative of the rationalism of the Enlightenment, the first to demonstrate its limitations. He dared to interrupt the songs of triumph of mere intellect. He showed that reason is the most valuable and the most specifically human power of man and yet is subject to the distorting effect of passions, and that only the understanding of man's passions can free his reason to function properly. He demonstrated the power as well as the weaknesses of human reason and made "the truth shall make you free" the guiding principle of a new therapy.

At first Freud thought that he was only concerned with certain forms of sickness and their cure. Slowly he became aware that he had gone far beyond the realm of medicine and had resumed a tradition in which psychology as the study of the soul of man was the theoretical basis for the art of living, for achieving happiness.

Freud's method, psychoanalysis, made possible the most minute and intimate study of the soul. The "laboratory" of the analyst has no gadgets. He cannot weigh or count his findings, but he gains insight through dreams, phantasies, and associations into the hidden desires and anxieties of his patients. In his "laboratory," relying only on observation, reason, and his own experience as a human being, he discovers that mental sickness cannot be understood apart from moral problems; that his patient is sick because he has neglected his soul's demands. The analyst is not a theologian or a philosopher and does not claim competence in those fields, but as a physician of the soul he is concerned with the very same problems as philosophy and theology: the soul of man and its cure.

If we thus define the function of the psychoanalyst we find that at present two professional groups are concerned with the soul: the priests and the psychoanalysts. What is their mutual relationship? Is the psychoanalyst trying to occupy the priest's domain and is opposition between them unavoidable? Or are they allies who work for the same ends and who should supplement and interpenetrate each other's field both theoretically and practically?

The former viewpoint has been expressed both by psychoanalysts and by representatives of the church. Freud's *The Future of an Illusion* [2] and Sheen's *Peace of Soul* [3] put the accent on opposition. C. G. Jung's [4] and Rabbi Liebman's [5] writings are characteristic of attempts to reconcile psychoanalysis and religion. The fact that a considerable number of ministers study psychoanalysis indicates how far this

2. Liveright Publishing Corporation, 1949.

3. An illustration of the unfortunate manner in which the subject matter is sometimes treated is a statement by Monsignor Sheen in his *Peace of Soul* (Whittlesey House, 1949). He writes: "When Freud wrote the following, he imposed an irrational prejudice on a theory: 'The mask is fallen: it [psychoanalysis] leads to a denial of God and of an ethical ideal.' " (Freud, *The Future of an Illusion*, p. 64.) Monsignor Sheen gives the impression that the statement he quotes is Freud's own opinion. If one looks up Freud's statement, however, one sees that the sentence quoted comes after the following: "If I now come forward with such displeasing statements, *people will be only too ready to displace their feelings from my person on to psycho-analysis. Now one can see, it will be said, where psycho-analysis leads to.* [Italics mine. E.F.] The mask is fallen; it leads to the denial of God and of an ethical ideal, as indeed we have always supposed. To keep us from the discovery, we have been made to believe that psycho-analysis neither has, nor can have, a philosophical standpoint." It is clear that Freud instead of expressing his own view refers to how people will attack psychoanalysis. The distortion lies in the fact that Freud is supposed to deny not only God but also an ethical ideal. While the first is true, the second is contrary to Freud's position. It is certainly Monsignor Sheen's privilege to believe that a denial of God leads to a denial of ethical ideals but not to make it appear as if this were Freud's own opinion. Had Monsignor Sheen even quoted the sentence correctly in a technical sense by keeping the words "as we have always supposed" or by indicating their omission, the reader would not have been so easily misled.

4. *Psychology and Religion* (Yale University Press, 1938).

5. *Peace of Mind* (Simon & Schuster, 1946)

belief in the blending of psychoanalysis and religion has penetrated the field of ministerial practice.

If I undertake to discuss the problem of religion and psychoanalysis afresh in these chapters it is because I want to show that to set up alternatives of either irreconcilable opposition or identity of interest is fallacious; a thorough and dispassionate discussion can demonstrate that the relation between religion and psychoanalysis is too complex to be forced into either one of these simple and convenient attitudes.

I want to show in these pages that it is not true that we have to give up the concern for the soul if we do not accept the tenets of religion. The psychoanalyst is in a position to study the human reality behind religion as well as behind nonreligious symbol systems. He finds that the question is not whether man returns to religion and believes in God but whether he lives love and thinks truth. If he does so the symbol systems he uses are of secondary importance. If he does not they are of no importance.

II

FREUD AND JUNG

FREUD dealt with the problem of religion and
psychoanalysis in one of his most profound and
brilliant books, *The Future of an Illusion*. Jung, who
was the first psychoanalyst to understand that myth
and religious ideas are expressions of profound insights, has dealt with the same topic in the Terry
Lectures of 1937, published under the title *Psychology and Religion*.

If I now attempt to give a brief summary of the
position of both psychoanalysts it is with a threefold
purpose:

1. To indicate where the discussion of the problem stands now and to locate the point from which I
want to proceed.

2. To lay the groundwork for the following
chapters by discussing some of the fundamental concepts used by Freud and Jung.

3. A correction of the widely held view that
Freud is "against" and Jung "for" religion will permit us to see the fallacy of such oversimplifying
statements in this complex field and to discuss the
ambiguities in the meanings of "religion" and
"psychoanalysis."

What is Freud's position in regard to religion as
expressed in *The Future of an Illusion?*

For Freud, religion has its origin in man's helplessness in confronting the forces of nature outside and the instinctive forces within himself. Religion arises at an early stage of human development when man cannot yet use his reason to deal with these outer and inner forces and must repress them or manage them with the help of other affective forces. So instead of coping with these forces by means of reason he copes with them by "counter–affects," by other emotional forces, the functions of which are to suppress and control that which he is powerless to cope with rationally.

In this process man develops what Freud calls an "illusion," the material of which is taken from his own individual experience as a child. Being confronted with dangerous, uncontrollable, and ununderstandable forces within and outside of himself, he remembers, as it were, and regresses to an experience he had as a child, when he felt protected by a father whom he thought to be of superior wisdom and strength, and whose love and protection he could win by obeying his commands and avoiding transgression of his prohibitions.

Thus religion, according to Freud, is a repetition of the experience of the child. Man copes with threatening forces in the same manner in which, as a child, he learned to cope with his own insecurity by relying on and admiring and fearing his father. Freud compares religion with the obsessional neuroses we find in children. And, according to him, religion is a collective neurosis, caused by conditions similar to those producing childhood neurosis.

Freud's analysis of the psychological roots of re-

ligion attempts to show *why* people formulated the
idea of a god. But it claims to do more than to get
at these psychological roots. It claims that the un-
reality of the theistic concept is demonstrated by ex-
posing it as an illusion based on man's wishes.[1]

Freud goes beyond attempting to prove that religion is an *illusion.* He says religion is a *danger* because it tends to sanctify bad human institutions with
which it has allied itself throughout its history; further, by teaching people to believe in an illusion and
by prohibiting critical thinking religion is responsible for the impoverishment of intelligence.[2] This
charge like the first one was leveled against the church
by the thinkers of the Enlightenment. But in Freud's
frame of reference this second charge is even more
potent than it was in the eighteenth century. Freud
could show in his analytic work that the prohibition
of critical thinking at one point leads to an impoverishment of a person's critical ability in other spheres

1. Freud himself states that the fact that an idea satisfies a wish
does not mean *necessarily* that the idea is false. Since psychoanalysts have sometimes made this erroneous conclusion, I want to
stress this remark of Freud's. Indeed, there are many true ideas
as well as false ones which man has arrived at because he wishes
the idea to be true. Most great discoveries are born out of interest
in finding something to be true. While the presence of such interest
may make the observer suspicious, it can never disprove the
validity of a concept or statement. The criterion of validity does
not lie in the psychological analysis of motivation but in the
examination of evidence for or against a hypothesis within a
logical framework of the hypothesis.

2. He points to the contrast between the brilliant intelligence
of a child and the impoverishment of reason in the average adult
(*Denkschwäche*). He suggests that the "innermost nature" of man
may not be as irrational as man becomes under the influence of
irrational teachings.

of thought and thereby impedes the power of reason. Freud's third objection to religion is that it puts morality on very shaky grounds. If the validity of ethical norms rests upon their being God's commands, the future of ethics stands or falls with the belief in God. Since Freud assumes that religious belief is on the wane he is forced to assume that the continued connection of religion and ethics will lead to the destruction of our moral values.

The dangers which Freud sees in religion make it apparent that his own ideals and values are the very things he considers to be threatened by religion: reason, reduction of human suffering, and morality. But we do not have to rely on inferences from Freud's criticism of religion; he has expressed very explicitly what are the norms and ideals he believes in: brotherly love (*Menschenliebe*), truth, and freedom. Reason and freedom are interdependent according to Freud. If man gives up his illusion of a fatherly God, if he faces his aloneness and insignificance in the universe, he will be like a child that has left his father's house. But it is the very aim of human development to overcome this infantile fixation. Man must educate himself to face reality. If he knows that he has nothing to rely on except his own powers, he will learn to use them properly. Only the free man who has emancipated himself from authority—authority that threatens and protects—can make use of his power of reason and grasp the world and his role in it objectively, without illusion but also with the ability to develop and to make use of the capacities inherent in him. Only if we grow up and cease to be children dependent on and afraid of authority can we dare to think for ourselves; but the reverse is also true. Only if we dare to think can we emancipate ourselves from domination by authority. It is significant in this context to note that Freud states that the feeling of powerlessness is the opposite of religious feeling. In view of the fact that many theologians—and, as we shall see later, Jung too to a certain extent—consider the feeling of dependence and powerlessness the core of religious experience, Freud's statement is very important. It is expressive, even though only by implication, of his own concept of religious experience, namely, that of independence and the awareness of one's powers. I shall attempt to show later on that this difference constitutes one of the critical problems in the psychology of religion.

Turning now to Jung we find at almost every point the opposite of Freud's views on religion.

Jung begins with a discussion of the general principles of his approach. While Freud, though not a professional philosopher, approaches the problem from a psychological *and* philosophical angle as William James, Dewey, and Macmurray have done, Jung states in the beginning of his book: "I restrict myself to the observation of phenomena and I refrain from any application of metaphysical or philosophical considerations." [3] He then goes on to explain how, as a psychologist, he can analyze religion without application of philosophical considerations. He calls

3. *Psychology and Religion*, p. 2.

his standpoint "phenomenological, that is, it is concerned with occurrences, events, experiences, in a
word, with facts. Its truth is a fact and not a judgment. Speaking for instance of the motive of the vir-
gin birth, psychology is only concerned with the fact
that there is such an idea, but it is not concerned with
the question whether such an idea is true or false in
any other sense. *It is psychologically true in as much
as it exists.* Psychological existence is subjective in
so far as an idea occurs in only one individual. But
it is objective in so far as it is established by a society—by a consensus gentium." [4]

Before I present Jung's analysis of religion a
critical examination of these methodological premises
seems warranted. Jung's use of the concept of truth
is not tenable. He states that "truth is a fact and not
a judgment," that "an elephant is true because it
exists." [5] But he forgets that truth always and necessarily refers to a judgment and not to a description
of a phenomenon which we perceive with our senses
and which we denote with a word symbol. Jung then
states that an idea is "psychologically true in as much
as it exists." But an idea "exists" regardless of
whether it is a delusion or whether it corresponds to
fact. The existence of an idea does not make it "true"
in any sense. Even the practicing psychiatrist could
not work were he not concerned with the truth of an
idea, that is, with its relation to the phenomena it
tends to portray. Otherwise he could not speak of a

4. *Ibid.,* p. 3. My italics.
5. *Ibid.,* p. 3.

delusion or a paranoid system. But Jung's approach
is not only untenable from a psychiatric standpoint;
he advocates a standpoint of relativism which, though
on the surface more friendly to religion than Freud's,
is in its spirit fundamentally opposed to religions like
Judaism, Christianity, and Buddhism. These consider the striving for truth as one of man's cardinal
virtues and obligations and insist that their doctrines
whether arrived at by revelation or only by the power
of reason are subject to the criterion of truth.

Jung does not fail to see the difficulties of his own
position, but the way in which he tries to solve them
is unfortunately equally untenable. He tries to differentiate between "subjective" and "objective" existence, in spite of the notoriously slippery quality of
these terms. Jung seems to mean that something objective is more valid and true than something that is
merely subjective. His criterion for the difference
between subjective and objective depends on whether
an idea occurs only to one individual or is established
by a society. But have we not been witnesses ourselves
of a "*folie à millions*," of the madness of whole groups
in our own age? Have we not seen that millions of
people, misguided by their irrational passions, can believe in ideas which are not less delusional and irrational than the products of a single individual?
What meaning is there in saying that they are "objective"? The spirit of this criterion for subjective
and objective is that of the same relativism which I
commented on above. More specifically, it is a so-
ciological relativism which makes social acceptance of

an idea the criterion of its validity, truth, or "objectivity." [6]

After discussing his methodological premises, Jung presents his views on the central problem: What is religion? What is the nature of religious experience? His definition is one which he shares with many theologians. It can be summarized briefly in the statement that the essence of religious experience is the submission to powers higher than ourselves. But we had better quote Jung directly. He states that religion "is a careful and scrupulous observation of what Rudolph Otto aptly termed the 'numinosum,' that is, a dynamic existence or effect, not caused by an arbitrary act of will. On the contrary, *it seizes and controls the human subject which is always rather its victim than its creator.*" [7]

Having defined religious experience as being seized by a power outside of ourselves, Jung proceeds to interpret the concept of the unconscious as being a religious one. According to him, the unconscious cannot be merely a part of the individual mind but is a power beyond our control intruding upon our minds. "The fact that you perceive the voice [of the unconscious] in your dream proves nothing at all, for you can also hear the voices in the street, which you would not explain as your own. There is only one condition under which you might legitimately call the voice your own, namely, when you assume your conscious personality

6. Cf. the discussion of universal versus socially immanent ethics in E. Fromm, *Man for Himself* (Rinehart and Company, 1947), pp. 237–244.

7. Jung, *Psychology and Religion*, p. 4. Italics mine.

to be a part of a whole or to be a smaller circle con-
tained in a bigger one. A little bank clerk, showing a
friend around town, who points out the bank build-
ing, saying, 'And here is *my* bank,' is using the same
privilege." [8]

It is a necessary consequence of his definition of
religion and of the unconscious that Jung arrives at
the conclusion that, in view of the nature of the unconscious mind, the influence of the unconscious upon
us "is a basic religious phenomenon." [9] It follows
that religious dogma and the dream are both religious
phenomena because they both are expressions of our
being seized by a power outside ourselves. Needless
to say, in the logic of Jung's thinking insanity would
have to be called an eminently religious phenomenon.

Does our examination of Freud's and Jung's attitudes toward religion bear out the popularly held
opinion that Freud is a foe and Jung a friend of
religion? A brief comparison of their views shows that
this assumption is a misleading oversimplification.

Freud holds that the aim of human development is
the achievement of these ideals: knowledge (reason,
truth, *logos*), brotherly love, reduction of suffering,
independence, and responsibility. These constitute
the ethical core of all great religions on which Eastern
and Western culture are based, the teachings of Con-
fucius and Lao-tse, Buddha, the Prophets and Jesus.
While there are certain differences of accent among
these teachings, e.g., Buddha emphasizing reduction

8. *Ibid.*, p. 47.
9. *Ibid.*, p. 46.

of suffering, the Prophets stressing knowledge and justice, and Jesus brotherly love, it is remarkable to what extent these religious teachers are in fundamental agreement about the aim of human development and the norms which ought to guide man. Freud speaks in the name of the ethical core of religion and criticizes the theistic-supernatural aspects of religion for preventing the full realization of these ethical aims. He explains the theistic-supernatural concepts as stages in human development which once were necessary and furthering but which now are no longer necessary and are in fact a barrier to further growth. The statement that Freud is "against" religion therefore is misleading unless we define sharply *what* religion or what aspects of religion he is critical of and what aspects of religion he speaks for.

For Jung, religious experience is characterized by a specific kind of emotional experience: surrender to a higher power, whether this higher power is called God or the unconscious. Undoubtedly this is a true characterization of a certain type of religious experience—in Christian religions, for instance, it is the core of Luther's or Calvin's teachings—while it contrasts with another type of religious experience, the one, for instance, which is represented by Buddhism. In its relativism concerning truth, however, Jung's concept of religion is in contrast to Buddhism, Judaism, and Christianity. In these, man's obligation to search for the truth is an integral postulate. Pilate's ironical question "What is truth?" stands as a symbol of an antireligious attitude from the standpoint not only of

Christianity but of all other great religions as well.

Summing up the respective positions of Freud and Jung we may say that Freud opposes religion in the name of ethics—an attitude which can be termed "religious." On the other hand, Jung reduces religion to a psychological phenomenon and at the same time elevates the unconscious to a religious phenomenon.[10]

10. It is interesting to note that Jung's position in *Psychology and Religion* is in many ways anticipated by William James, while Freud's position is in essential points similar to that taken by John Dewey. William James calls this religious attitude "both a helpless and a sacrificial attitude . . . which the individual finds himself impelled to take up towards what he apprehends to be the divine." (*The Varieties of Religious Experience* [Modern Library], p. 51.) Like Jung he compares the unconscious with the God concept of the theologian. He says: "At the same time the theologian's contention that the religious man is moved by an external power is vindicated, for it is one of the peculiarities of invasions from the subconscious region to take on objective appearances, and to suggest to the Subject an external control." (*loc. cit.* p. 503.) In this connection between the unconscious (or, in James's terminology, the subconscious) and God, James sees the link between religion and the science of psychology.

John Dewey differentiates religion and religious experience. To him the supernatural dogmas of religion have weakened and sapped man's religious attitude. "The opposition between religious values as I conceive them," he says, "and religions is not to be bridged. Just because the release of these values is so important, their identification with the creeds and cults of religions must be dissolved." (*A Common Faith* [Yale University Press, 1934], p. 28.) Like Freud he states: "Men have never fully used the powers they possess to advance the good in life, because they have waited upon some power external to themselves and to nature to do the work they are responsible for doing." (*loc. cit.,* p. 46.) Consult also John Macmurray's position in *The Structure of Religious Experience* (Yale University Press, 1936). He stresses the difference between rational and irrational, sentimental and vicious religious emotions. In contrast to the relativistic position Jung takes, he states: "No reflective activity can be justified except in so far as it achieves truth and validity, and escapes error and falsity." (*loc. cit.,* p. 54.)

III

AN ANALYSIS OF SOME TYPES OF
RELIGIOUS EXPERIENCE

ANY discussion of religion is handicapped by a serious terminological difficulty. While we know that there were and are many religions outside of monotheism, we nevertheless associate the concept religion with a system centered around God and supernatural forces; we tend to consider monotheistic religion as a frame of reference for the understanding and evaluation of all other religions. It thus becomes doubtful whether religions without God like Buddhism, Taoism, or Confucianism can be properly called religions. Such secular systems as contemporary authoritarianism are not called religions at all, although psychologically speaking they deserve this name. We simply have no word to denote religion as a general human phenomenon in such a way that some association with a specific type of religion does not creep in and color the concept. For lack of such a word I shall use the term religion in these chapters, but I want to make it clear at the outset that I understand by religion *any system of thought and action shared by a group which gives the individual a frame of orientation and an object of devotion.*

There is indeed no culture of the past, and it seems there can be no culture in the future, which does not have religion in this broad sense of our definition.

We need not, however, stop at this merely descriptive statement. The study of man permits us to recognize that the need for a common system of orientation and for an object of devotion is deeply rooted in the conditions of human existence. I have attempted in *Man for Himself* to analyze the nature of this need, and I quote from that book:

"Self-awareness, reason, and imagination have disrupted the 'harmony' which characterizes animal existence. Their emergence has made man into an anomaly, into the freak of the universe. He is part of nature, subject to her physical laws and unable to change them, yet he transcends the rest of nature. He is set apart while being a part; he is homeless, yet chained to the home he shares with all creatures. Cast into this world at an accidental place and time, he is forced out of it, again accidentally. Being aware of himself, he realizes his powerlessness and the limitations of his existence. He visualizes his own end: death. Never is he free from the dichotomy of his existence: he cannot rid himself of his mind, even if he should want to; he cannot rid himself of his body as long as he is alive—and his body makes him want to be alive.

"Reason, man's blessing, is also his curse; it forces him to cope everlastingly with the task of solving an insoluble dichotomy. Human existence is different in this respect from that of all other organisms; it is in a state of constant and unavoidable disequilibrium. Man's life cannot 'be lived' by repeating the pattern of his species; *he* must live. Man is the only animal that can be *bored*, that can be *discontented*, that can feel evicted from paradise. Man is the only animal for whom his own existence is a problem which he has to solve and from which he cannot escape. He cannot go back to the prehuman state of harmony with nature; he must proceed to develop his reason until he becomes the master of nature, and of himself.

"The emergence of reason has created a dichotomy within man which forces him to strive everlastingly for new solutions. The dynamism of his history is intrinsic to the existence of reason which causes him to develop and, through it, to create a world of his own in which he can feel at home with himself and his fellow men. Every stage he reaches leaves him discontented and perplexed, and this very perplexity urges him to move toward new solutions. There is no innate 'drive for progress' in man; it is the contradiction in his existence that makes him proceed on the way he set out. Having lost paradise, the unity with nature, he has become the eternal wanderer (Odysseus, Oedipus, Abraham, Faust); he is impelled to go forward and with everlasting effort to make the unknown known by filling in with answers the blank spaces of his knowledge. He must give account to himself of himself, and of the meaning of his existence. He is driven to overcome this inner split, tormented by a craving for 'absoluteness,' for another kind of harmony which can lift the curse by which he was separated from nature, from his fellow men, and from himself."

•   •   •   •   •

"The disharmony of man's existence generates needs which far transcend those of his animal origin. These needs result in an imperative drive to restore a unity and equilibrium between himself and the rest of nature. He makes the attempt to restore this unity and equilibrium in the first place in thought by constructing an all-inclusive mental picture of the world which serves as a frame of reference from which he can derive an answer to the question of where he stands and what he ought to do. But such thought-systems are not sufficient. If man were only a disembodied intellect his aim would be achieved by a comprehensive thought-system. But since he is an entity endowed with a body as well as a mind he has to react to the dichotomy of his existence not only in thinking but also in the process of living, in his feelings and actions. He has to strive for the experience of unity and oneness in all spheres of his being in order to find a new equilibrium. Hence any satisfying system of orientation implies not only intellectual elements but elements of feeling and sense to be realized in action in all fields of human endeavor. Devotion to an aim, or an idea, or a power transcending man such as God, is an expression of this need for completeness in the process of living."

. . . . .

"Because the need for a system of orientation and devotion is an intrinsic part of human existence we can understand the intensity of this need. Indeed, there is no other more powerful source of energy in man. Man is not free to choose between having or not having 'ideals,' but he is free to choose between different kinds of ideals, between being devoted to the worship of power and destruction and being devoted to reason and love. All men are 'idealists' and are striving for something beyond the attainment of physical satisfaction. They differ in the kinds of ideals they believe in. The very best but also the most satanic manifestations of man's mind are expressions not of his flesh but of his 'idealism,' of his spirit. Therefore a relativistic view which claims that to have some ideal or some religious feeling is valuable in itself is dangerous and erroneous. We must understand every ideal including those which appear in secular ideologies as expressions of the same human need and we must judge them with respect to their truth, to the extent to which they are conducive to the unfolding of man's powers and to the degree to which they are a real answer to man's need for equilibrium and harmony in his world." [1]

What I have said about man's idealism holds true equally for his religious need. There is no one without a religious need, a need to have a frame of orientation and an object of devotion; but this statement does not tell us anything about a specific context in which this religious need is manifest. Man may worship animals, trees, idols of gold or stone, an invisible god, a saintly man or diabolic leaders; he may worship his ancestors, his nation, his class or party, money or success; his religion may be conducive to the development of

1. *Man for Himself,* pp. 40–41, 46–47, 49–50.

destructiveness or of love, of domination or of brother-liness; it may further his power of reason or paralyze it; he may be aware of his system as being a religious one, different from those of the secular realm, or he may think that he has no religion and interpret his devotion to certain allegedly secular aims like power, money or success as nothing but his concern for the practical and expedient. The question is not *religion or not* but *which kind of religion*, whether it is one furthering man's development, the unfolding of his specifically human powers, or one paralyzing them.

Curiously enough the interests of the devoted re-ligionist and of the psychologist are the same in this respect. The theologian is keenly interested in the specific tenets of a religion, his own and others, be-cause what matters to him is the truth of his belief against the others. Equally, the psychologist must be keenly interested in the specific contents of religion for what matters to him is what human attitude a re-ligion expresses and what kind of effect it has on man, whether it is good or bad for the development of man's powers. He is interested not only in an analysis of the *psychological roots* of various religions but also in their *value*.

The thesis that the need for a frame of orientation and an object of devotion is rooted in the conditions of man's existence seems to be amply verified by the fact of the universal occurrence of religion in history. This point has been made and elaborated by theolo-gians, psychologists, and anthropologists, and there is no need for me to discuss it any further. I only want to stress that in making this point the adherents of traditional religion have often indulged in a fallacious bit of reasoning. Starting out with so broad a definition of religion as to include every possible religious phenomenon, their concept has remained associated with monotheistic religion, and thus they proceed to look upon all nonmonotheistic forms as precursors of or deviations from the "true" religion and they end demonstrating that the belief in God in the sense of the Western religious tradition is inherent in man's equipment.

The psychoanalyst whose "laboratory" is the patient and who is a participant observer of another person's thoughts and feelings is able to add another proof to the fact that the need for some frame of orientation and object of devotion is inherent in man. In studying neuroses he discovers that he is studying religion. It was Freud who saw the connection between neurosis and religion; but while he interpreted religion as a collective childhood neurosis of mankind, the statement can also be reversed. We can interpret *neurosis as a private form of religion*, more specifically, as a regression to primitive forms of religion conflicting with officially recognized patterns of religious thought.

One can look at a neurosis from two aspects. One can focus on the neurotic phenomena themselves, the symptoms and other specific difficulties in living which the neurosis produces. The other aspect is not concerned with the positive as it were, with the neurosis, but with the negative, the failure of the neurotic individual to accomplish the fundamental aims of human existence, independence and the ability to be productive, to love, to think. Anyone who has failed to achieve maturity and integration develops a neurosis of one kind or another. He does not "just live," unbothered by this failure, satisfied to eat and drink, sleep and have sexual satisfaction and do his work; if this were the case then indeed we would have the proof that the religious attitude, while perhaps desirable, is not an intrinsic part of human nature. But the study of man shows that this is not so. If a person has not succeeded in integrating his energies in the direction of his higher self, he canalizes them in the direction of lower goals; if he has no picture of the world and his position in it which approximates the truth, he will create a picture which is illusory and cling to it with the same tenacity with which the religionist believes in his dogmas. Indeed, "man does not live by bread alone." He has only the choice of better or worse, higher or lower, satisfactory or destructive forms of religions and philosophies.

What is the religious situation in contemporary Western society? It resembles in curious fashion the picture which the anthropologist gets in studying the religion of the North American Indians. They have been converted to the Christian religion but their old pre-Christian religions have by no means been uprooted. Christianity is a veneer laid over this old religion and blended with it in many ways. In our own culture monotheistic religion and also atheistic and agnostic philosophies are a thin veneer built upon religions which are in many ways far more "primitive" than the Indian religions and, being sheer idolatry, are also more incompatible with the essential teachings of monotheism. As a collective and potent form of modern idolatry we find the worship of power, of success and of the authority of the market; but aside from these collective forms we find something else. If we scratch the surface of modern man we discover any number of individualized primitive forms of religion. Many of these are called neuroses, but one might just as well call them by their respective religious names: ancestor worship, totemism, fetishism, ritualism, the cult of cleanliness, and so on.

Do we actually find ancestor worship? Indeed, ancestor worship is one of the most widespread primitive cults in our society and it does not alter its picture if we call it, as the psychiatrist does, neurotic fixation to father or mother. Let us consider such a case of ancestor worship. A beautiful, highly talented woman, a painter, was attached to her father in such a way that she would refuse to have any close contact with men; she spent all her free time with her father, a pleasant but rather dull gentleman who had been widowed early. Aside from her painting, nothing but her father was of any interest to her. The picture she gave of him to others was grotesquely different from reality. After he died she committed suicide and left a will stipulating only that she was to be buried by his side.

Another person, a very intelligent and gifted man, highly respected by everyone, led a secret life completely devoted to the worship of his father who, viewed most charitably, could be described as a shrewd go-getter, interested solely in acquiring money and social prestige. The son's picture of the father was, however, that of the wisest, most loving, and devoted parent, ordained by God to show him the right way to live; the son's every action and thought was considered from the standpoint of whether his father would approve or not, and since in real life his father had usually disapproved, the patient felt "out of grace" most of the time and frantically attempted to regain his father's approval even many years after his father had died.

The psychoanalyst tries to discover the causes of such pathological attachments and hopes to help the patient to free himself from such crippling father worship. But we are not interested here in the causes or in the problem of cure but in the phenomenology. We find a dependency on a father enduring with undiminished intensity many years after the parent's death, which cripples the patient's judgment, renders him unable to love, makes him feel like a child, constantly insecure and frightened. This centering one's life around an ancestor, spending most of one's energy in his worship, is not different from a religious ancestor cult. It gives a frame of reference and a unifying principle of devotion. Here too is the reason the patient cannot be cured by simply pointing out the irrationality of his behavior and the damage he does to himself. He often knows this intellectually in one compartment of himself, as it were, but emotionally he is completely devoted to his cult. Only if a profound change in his total personality occurs, if he becomes free *to* think, *to* love, *to* attain a new focus of orientation and devotion, can he be free *from* the slavish devotion to his parent; only if he is capable of adopting a higher form of religion can he free himself from his lower form.

Compulsive neurotic patients exhibit numerous forms of private ritual. The person whose life is centered around the feeling of guilt and the need for atonement may choose a washing compulsion as the dominant ritual of his life; another whose compulsion is exhibited in thinking rather than actions will have a ritual which forces him to think or say certain formulas which are supposed to avert disaster and others which are supposed to guarantee success. Whether we call these neurotic symptoms or ritual depends on our point of view; in substance these symptoms *are* rituals of a private religion.

Do we have totemism in our culture? We have a great deal—although the people suffering from it usually do not consider themselves in need of psychiatric help. A person whose exclusive devotion is to the state or his political party, whose only criterion of value and truth is the interest of state or party, for whom the flag as a symbol of his group is a holy object, has a religion of clan and totem worship, even though in his own eyes it is a perfectly rational system (which, of course, all devotees to any kind of primitive religion believe). If we want to understand how systems like fascism or Stalinism can possess millions of people, ready to sacrifice their integrity and reason to the principle, "my country, right or wrong," we are forced to consider the totemistic, the religious quality of their orientation.

Another form of private religion, very widespread although not dominant in our culture, is the religion of cleanliness. The adherents of this religion have one major standard of value according to which they judge people—cleanliness and orderliness. The phenomenon was strikingly apparent in the reaction of many American soldiers during the last war. Often at odds with their political convictions, they judged allies and enemies from the standpoint of this religion. The English and the Germans ranked high, the French and Italians low in this scale of values. This religion of cleanliness and orderliness is, in substance, not too different from certain highly ritualistic religious systems which are centered around the attempt to get rid of evil by cleansing rituals and to find security in the strict performance of ritualistic orderliness.

There is one important difference between a religious cult and neurosis which makes the cult vastly superior to the neurosis as far as the satisfaction gained is concerned. If we imagine that the patient with his neurotic fixation to his father lived in a culture where ancestor worship is generally practiced as a cult, he could share his feelings with his fellow men rather than feel himself isolated. And it is the feeling of isolation, of being shut-out, which is the painful sting of every neurosis. Even the most irrational orientation if it is shared by a considerable body of men gives the individual the feeling of oneness with others, a certain amount of security and stability which the neurotic person lacks. There is nothing inhuman, evil, or irrational which does not give some comfort provided it is shared by a group. The most convincing proof for this statement can be found in those incidents of mass madness of which we have been and still are witnesses. Once a doctrine, however irrational, has gained power in a society, millions of people will believe in it rather than feel ostracized and isolated.

These ideas lead to an important consideration concerning the function of religion. If man regresses so easily into a more primitive form of religion, have not the monotheistic religions today the function of saving man from such regression? Is not the belief in God a safeguard against falling back into ancestor, totem, or golden-calf worship? Indeed, this would be so if religion had succeeded in molding man's character according to its stated ideals. But historical religion has capitulated before and compromised with secular power again and again. It has been concerned far more with certain dogmas rather than with the practice of love and humility in everyday life. It has failed to challenge secular power relentlessly and unceasingly where such power has violated the spirit of the religious ideal; on the contrary, it has shared again and again in such violations. If the churches were the representatives not only of the words but of the spirit of the Ten Commandments or of the Golden Rule, they could be potent forces blocking the regression to idol worship. But since this is an exception rather than the rule, the question must be asked, not from an antireligious point of view but out of concern for man's soul: Can we trust religion to be the representative of religious needs or must we not separate these needs from organized, traditional religion in order to prevent the collapse of our moral structure?

In considering an answer to this question we must remember that no intelligent discussion of the problem is possible as long as we deal with religion in general instead of differentiating between various types of religion and religious experience. It would far transcend the scope of this chapter to attempt a review of all types of religion. Even to discuss only those types which are relevant from the psychological standpoint cannot be undertaken here. I shall therefore deal with only one distinction, but one which in my opinion is the most important, and which cuts across nontheistic and theistic religions: that between *authoritarian* and *humanistic* religions.

What is the principle of authoritarian religion? The definition of religion given in the *Oxford Dictionary*, while attempting to define religion as such, is a rather accurate definition of authoritarian religion. It reads: "[Religion is] recognition on the part of man of some higher unseen power as having control of his destiny, and as being entitled to obedience, reverence, and worship."

Here the emphasis is on the recognition that man is controlled by a higher power outside of himself.

But this alone does not constitute authoritarian religion. What makes it so is the idea that this power, because of the control it exercises, is *entitled* to "obedience, reverence and worship." I italicize the word "entitled" because it shows that the reason for worship, obedience, and reverence lies not in the moral qualities of the deity, not in love or justice, but in the fact that it has control, that is, has power over man. Furthermore it shows that the higher power has a right to force man to worship him and that lack of reverence and obedience constitutes sin.

The essential element in authoritarian religion and in the authoritarian religious experience is the surrender to a power transcending man. The main virtue of this type of religion is obedience, its cardinal sin is disobedience. Just as the deity is conceived as omnipotent or omniscient, man is conceived as being powerless and insignificant. Only as he can gain grace or help from the deity by complete surrender can he feel strength. Submission to a powerful authority is one of the avenues by which man escapes from his feeling of aloneness and limitation. In the act of surrender he loses his independence and integrity as an individual but he gains the feeling of being protected by an awe-inspiring power of which, as it were, he becomes a part.

In Calvin's theology we find a vivid picture of authoritarian, theistic thinking. "For I do not call it humility," says Calvin, "if you suppose that we have anything left. . . . We cannot think of ourselves as we ought to think without utterly despising everything that may be supposed an excellence in us. This humility is unfeigned submission of a mind overwhelmed with a weighty sense of its own misery and poverty; for such is the uniform description of it in the word of God." [2]

The experience which Calvin describes here, that of despising everything in oneself, of the submission of the mind overwhelmed by its own poverty, is the very essence of all authoritarian religions whether they are couched in secular or in theological language.[3] In authoritarian religion God is a symbol of power and force, He is supreme because He has supreme power, and man in juxtaposition is utterly powerless.

Authoritarian secular religion follows the same principle. Here the Führer or the beloved "Father of His People" or the State or the Race or the Socialist Fatherland becomes the object of worship; the life of the individual becomes insignificant and man's worth consists in the very denial of his worth and strength. Frequently authoritarian religion postulates an ideal which is so abstract and so distant that it has hardly any connection with the real life of real people. To such ideals as "life after death" or "the future of mankind" the life and happiness of persons living here and now may be sacrificed; the alleged ends justify every means and become symbols in the

2. Johannes Calvin, *Institutes of the Christian Religion* (Presbyterian Board of Christian Education, 1928), p. 681.

3. See Erich Fromm, *Escape from Freedom* (Farrar & Rinehart, 1941), pp. 141 ff. This attitude toward authority is described there in detail.

names of which religious or secular "elites" control the lives of their fellow men.

Humanistic religion, on the contrary, is centered around man and his strength. Man must develop his power of reason in order to understand himself, his relationship to his fellow men and his position in the universe. He must recognize the truth, both with regard to his limitations and his potentialities. He must develop his powers of love for others as well as for himself and experience the solidarity of all living beings. He must have principles and norms to guide him in this aim. Religious experience in this kind of religion is the experience of oneness with the All, based on one's relatedness to the world as it is grasped with thought and with love. Man's aim in humanistic religion is to achieve the greatest strength, not the greatest powerlessness; virtue is self-realization, not obedience. Faith is certainty of conviction based on one's experience of thought and feeling, not assent to propositions on credit of the proposer. The prevailing mood is that of joy, while the prevailing mood in authoritarian religion is that of sorrow and of guilt.

Inasmuch as humanistic religions are theistic, God is a symbol of *man's own powers* which he tries to realize in his life, and is not a symbol of force and domination, having *power over man*.

Illustrations of humanistic religions are early Buddhism, Taoism, the teachings of Isaiah, Jesus, Socrates, Spinoza, certain trends in the Jewish and Christian religions (particularly mysticism), the religion of Reason of the French Revolution. It is evident from these that the distinction between authoritarian and humanistic religion cuts across the distinction between theistic and nontheistic, and between religions in the narrow sense of the word and philosophical systems of religious character. What matters in all such systems is not the thought system as such but the human attitude underlying their doctrines.

One of the best examples of humanistic religions is early Buddhism. The Buddha is a great teacher, he is the "awakened one" who recognizes the truth about human existence. He does not speak in the name of a supernatural power but in the name of reason. He calls upon every man to make use of his own reason and to see the truth which he was only the first to find. Once man takes the first step in seeing the truth, he must apply his efforts to live in such a way that he develops his powers of reason and of love for all human creatures. Only to the degree to which he succeeds in this can he free himself from the bondage of irrational passions. While man must recognize his limitations according to Buddhistic teaching, he must also become aware of the powers in himself. The concept of Nirvana as the state of mind the fully awakened one can achieve is not one of man's helplessness and submission but on the contrary one of the development of the highest powers man possesses.

The following story of Buddha is very characteristic.

Once a hare sat under a mango tree and slept. Suddenly he heard a loud noise. He thought the world was coming to an end and started to run. When the other hares saw him running they asked, "Why do you run so fast?" He replied, "The world is coming to an end." Upon hearing this they all joined him in his flight. When the deer saw the hares running they asked them, "Why do you run so fast?" and the hares answered, "We run because the world is coming to an end." Upon which the deer joined them in their flight. Thus one species after another joined the animals already running until the whole animal kingdom was in a panicky flight which would have ended in its destruction. When Buddha, who at that time was living as a wise man, one of his many forms of existence, saw all the animals running in their panic he asked the last group that had joined the flight why they were running. "Because the world is coming to an end," they answered. "This cannot be true," Buddha said. "The world is not coming to an end. Let us find out why they think so." He then inquired of one species after another, tracing the rumor back to the deer and then at last to the hares. When the hares told him that they were running because the world was coming to an end, he asked which particular hare had told them so. They pointed to the one who had started the report, and Buddha turned to him and asked, "Where were you and what did you do when you thought the world was coming to an end?" The hare answered, "I was sitting under a mango tree and was asleep." "You probably heard a mango fruit fall," Buddha told him. "The noise awakened you, you got frightened and thought the world was coming to an end. Let

us go back to the tree where you sat and find out
whether this was so." They both went to the tree.
They found that indeed a mango had fallen where the
hare had sat. Thus Buddha saved the animal kingdom
from destruction.

I quote this story not primarily because it is one
of the earliest examples of analytic inquiry into the
origins of fright and rumors but because it is so expressive of the Buddhistic spirit. It shows loving concern for the creatures of the animal world and at the
same time penetrating, rational understanding and
confidence in man's powers.

Zen-Buddhism, a later sect within Buddhism, is expressive of an even more radical anti-authoritarian
attitude. Zen proposes that no knowledge is of any
value unless it grows out of ourselves; no authority,
no teacher can really teach us anything except to
arouse doubts in us; words and thought systems are
dangerous because they easily turn into authorities
whom we worship. Life itself must be grasped and experienced as it flows, and in this lies virtue. Characteristic of this unauthoritarian attitude toward
supreme beings is the following story:

"When Tanka of the T'ang dynasty stopped at
Yerinji in the Capitol, it was severely cold; so taking
down one of the Buddha images enshrined there, he
made a fire of it and warmed himself. The keeper of
the shrine, seeing this, was greatly incensed, and ex-
claimed: 'How dare you burn my wooden image of the
Buddha?'

"Tanka began to search in the ashes as if he were looking for something, and said: 'I am gathering the holy sariras [a kind of mineral deposit found in the human body after cremation and believed to correspond to the saintliness of life] from the burnt ashes.'

" 'How,' said the keeper, 'can you get sariras from a wooden Buddha?'

"Tanka retorted, 'If there are no sariras to be found in it, may I have the remaining two Buddhas for my fire?'

"The shrine-keeper later lost both his eyebrows for remonstrating against this apparent impiety of Tanka, while the Buddha's wrath never fell on the latter." [4]

Another illustration of a humanistic religious system is to be found in Spinoza's religious thinking. While his language is that of medieval theology, his concept of God has no trace of authoritarianism. God could not have created the world different from what it is. He cannot change anything; in fact, God is identical with the totality of the universe. Man must see his own limitations and recognize that he is dependent on the totality of forces outside himself over which

4. D. T. Suzuki, *An Introduction to Zen Buddhism* (Rider and Company, 1948), p. 124. Cf. also Professor Suzuki's other works on Zen, and Ch. Humphrey, *Zen Buddhism* (W. Heinemann, Ltd., 1949). An anthology of religious documents expressive of humanistic religion, drawn from all the great sources of the East and West, edited by Victor Gollancz, will be published this year. Here the reader will find a wealth of documentation on humanistic religious thinking.

he has no control. Yet his are the powers of love and of reason. He can develop them and attain an optimum of freedom and of inner strength.

The distinction between authoritarian and humanistic religion not only cuts across various religions, it can exist within the same religion. Our own religious tradition is one of the best illustrations of this point. Since it is of fundamental importance to understand fully the distinction between authoritarian and humanistic religion I shall illustrate it further from a source with which every reader is more or less familiar, the Old Testament.

The beginning of the Old Testament [5] is written in the spirit of authoritarian religion. The picture of God is that of the absolute ruler of a patriarchal clan, who has created man at his pleasure and can destroy him at will. He has forbidden him to eat from the tree of knowledge of good and evil and has threatened him with death if he transgresses this order. But the serpent, "more clever than any animal," tells Eve, "Ye shall not surely die: For God doth know that in the day ye eat thereof, then your eyes shall be opened, and ye shall be as gods, knowing good and evil." [6] God proves the serpent to be right. When Adam and Eve have transgressed he punishes them by proclaiming enmity between man and nature, between man and the soil and animals, and between men and women. But

5. The historical fact that the beginning of the Bible may not be its oldest part does not need to be considered here since we use the text as an illustration of two principles and not to establish a historical sequence.

6. Genesis 3:4–5.

man is not to die. However, "the man has become as one of us, to know good and evil: and now, lest he put forth his hand, and take also of the tree of life, and eat, and live for ever," [7] God expells Adam and Eve from the garden of Eden and puts an angel with a flaming sword at the east "to keep the way of the tree of life."

The text makes very clear what man's sin is: it is rebellion against God's command; it is disobedience and not any inherent sinfulness in the act of eating from the tree of knowledge. On the contrary, further religious development has made the knowledge of good and evil the cardinal virtue to which man may aspire. The text also makes it plain what God's motive is: it is concern with his own superior role, the jealous fear of man's claim to become his equal.

A decisive turning point in the relationship between God and man is to be seen in the story of the Flood. When God saw "that the wickedness of man was great on the earth . . . it repented the Lord that he had made man and the earth, and it grieved him at his heart. And the Lord said, I will destroy man whom I have created from the face of the earth; both man, and beast, and the creeping thing, and the fowls of the air; for it repenteth me that I have made them." [8]

There is no question here but that God has the right to destroy his own creatures; he has created them and they are his property. The text defines their

7. *Ibid.* 3: 22.
8. *Ibid.* 6: 5 ff.

wickedness as "violence," but the decision to destroy
not only man but animals and plants as well shows
that we are not dealing here with a sentence com-
mensurate with some specific crime but with God's
angry regret over his own action which did not turn
out well. "But Noah found grace in the eyes of the
Lord," and he, together with his family and a representative of each animal species, is saved from the
Flood. Thus far the destruction of man and the salvation of Noah are arbitrary acts of God. He could
do as he pleased, as can any powerful tribal chief. But
after the Flood the relationship between God and man
changes fundamentally. A covenant is concluded between God and man in which God promises that
"neither shall all flesh be cut off any more by the
waters of a flood; neither shall there any more be a
flood to destroy the earth." [9] God obligates himself
never to destroy all life on earth, and man is bound
to the first and most fundamental command of the
Bible, not to kill: "At the hand of every man's brother
will I require the life of man." [10] From this point on
the relationship between God and man undergoes a
profound change. God is no longer an absolute ruler
who can act at his pleasure but is bound by a constitution to which both he and man must adhere; he
is bound by a principle which he cannot violate, the
principle of respect for life. God can punish man if he
violates this principle, but man can also challenge
God if he is guilty of its violation.

9. *Ibid.* 9:11.
10. *Ibid.* 9:5.

The new relationship between God and man appears clearly in Abraham's plea for Sodom and Gomorrah. When God considers destroying the cities because of their wickedness, Abraham criticizes God for violating his own principles. "That be far from thee to do after this manner, to slay the righteous with the wicked: and that the righteous should be as the wicked, that be far from thee. Shall not the Judge of all the earth do right?" [11]

The difference between the story of the Fall and this argument is great indeed. There man is forbidden to know good and evil and his position toward God is that of submission—or sinful disobedience. Here man uses his knowledge of good and evil, criticizes God in the name of justice, and God has to yield.

Even this brief analysis of the authoritarian elements in the biblical story shows that at the root of the Judaeo-Christian religion both principles, the authoritarian and the humanistic, are present. In the development of Judaism as well as of Christianity both principles have been preserved and their respective preponderance marks different trends in the two religions.

The following story from the Talmud expresses the unauthoritarian, humanistic side of Judaism as we find it in the first centuries of the Christian era.

A number of other famous rabbinical scholars disagreed with Rabbi Eliezar's views in regard to a point

11. *Ibid.* 18:25.

of ritual law. "Rabbi Eliezar said to them: 'If the law is as I think it is then this tree shall let us know.' Whereupon the tree jumped from its place a hundred yards (others say four hundred yards). His colleagues said to him, 'One does not prove anything from a tree.' He said, 'If I am right then this brook shall let us know.' Whereupon the brook ran upstream. His colleagues said to him, 'One does not prove anything from a brook.' He continued and said, 'If the law is as I think then the walls of this house will tell.' Whereupon the walls began to fall. But Rabbi Joshua shouted at the walls and said, 'If scholars argue a point of law, what business have you to fall?' So the walls fell no further out of respect for Rabbi Joshua but out of respect for Rabbi Eliezar did not straighten up. And that is the way they still are. Rabbi Eliezar took up the argument again and said, 'If the law is as I think, they shall tell us from heaven.' Whereupon a voice from heaven said, 'What have you against Rabbi Eliezar, because the law is as he says.' Whereupon Rabbi Joshua got up and said, 'It is written in the Bible: The law is not in heaven. What does this mean? According to Rabbi Jirmijahu it means since the Torah has been given on Mount Sinai we no longer pay attention to voices from heaven because it is written: You make your decision according to the majority opinion.' It then happened that Rabbi Nathan [one of the participants in the discussion] met the Prophet Elijah [who had taken a stroll on earth] and he asked the Prophet, 'What did God himself say when we had this discussion?' The

Prophet answered, 'God smiled and said, My children have won, my children have won.' " [12]

This story is hardly in need of comment. It emphasizes the autonomy of man's reason with which even the supernatural voices from heaven cannot interfere. God smiles, man has done what God wanted him to do, he has become his own master, capable and resolved to make his decisions by himself according to rational, democratic methods.

The same humanistic spirit can be found in many stories from the Chassidic folklore of more than a thousand years later. The Chassidic movement was a rebellion of the poor against those who had the monopoly of learning or of money. Their motto was the verse of the Psalms: "Serve God in joy." They emphasized feeling rather than intellectual accomplishment, joy rather than contrition; to them (as to Spinoza) joy was the equivalent of virtue and sadness the equivalent of sin. The following story is characteristic of the humanistic and anti-authoritarian spirit of this religious sect:

A poor tailor came to a Chassidic rabbi the day after the Day of Atonement and said to him, "Yesterday I had an argument with God. I told him, 'Oh God, you have committed sins and I have committed sins. But you have committed grave sins and I have committed sins of no great importance. What have you done? You have separated mothers from their children and permitted people to starve. What have I done? I have sometimes failed to return a piece of

12. Talmud, Baba Meziah, 59, b. (My translation.)

cloth to a customer or have not been strict in the observance of the law. But I will tell you, God. I will forgive you your sins and you forgive me mine. Thus we are even.' " Whereupon the Rabbi answered, "You fool! Why did you let him get away that easily? Yesterday you could have forced him to send the Messiah."

This story demonstrates even more drastically than that of Abraham's argument with God the idea that God must live up to his promises just as man must live up to his. If God fails to put an end to the suffering of man as he has promised, man has the right to challenge him, in fact to force him to fulfill his promise. While the two stories quoted here are within the frame of reference of monotheistic religion, the human attitude behind them is profoundly different from that behind Abraham's readiness to sacrifice Isaac or Calvin's glorification of God's dictatorial powers.

That early Christianity is humanistic and not authoritarian is evident from the spirit and text of all Jesus' teachings. Jesus' precept that "the kingdom of God is within you" is the simple and clear expression of nonauthoritarian thinking. But only a few hundred years later, after Christianity had ceased to be the religion of the poor and humble peasants, artisans, and slaves (the *Am haarez*) and had become the religion of those ruling the Roman Empire, the authoritarian trend in Christianity became dominant. Even so, the conflict between the authoritarian and humanistic principles in Christianity never ceased. It was the conflict between Augustine and Pelagius, between the Catholic Church and the many "heretic" groups and between various sects within Protestantism. The humanistic, democratic element was never subdued in Christian or in Jewish history, and this element found one of its most potent expressions in the mystic thinking within both religions. The mystics have been deeply imbued with the experience of man's strength, his likeness to God, and with the idea that God needs man as much as man needs God; they have understood the sentence that man is created in the image of God to mean the fundamental identity of God and man. Not fear and submission but love and the assertion of one's own powers are the basis of mystical experience. *God is not a symbol of power over man but of man's own powers.*

Thus far we have dealt with the distinctive features of authoritarian and humanistic religions mainly in descriptive terms. But the psychoanalyst must proceed from the description of attitudes to the analysis of their dynamics, and it is here that he can contribute to our discussion from an area not accessible to other fields of inquiry. The full understanding of an attitude requires an appreciation of those conscious and, in particular, unconscious processes occurring in the individual which provide the necessity for and the conditions of its development.

While in humanistic religion God is the image of man's higher self, a symbol of what man potentially is or ought to become, in authoritarian religion God becomes the sole possessor of what was originally man's: of his reason and his love. The more perfect God becomes, the more imperfect becomes man. He *projects* the best he has onto God and thus impoverishes himself. Now God has all love, all wisdom, all justice—and man is deprived of these qualities, he is empty and poor. He had begun with the feeling of smallness, but he now has become completely powerless and without strength; all his powers have been projected onto God. This mechanism of projection is the very same which can be observed in interpersonal relationships of a masochistic, submissive character, where one person is awed by another and attributes his own powers and aspirations to the other person. It is the same mechanism that makes people endow the leaders of even the most inhuman systems with qualities of superwisdom and kindness.[13]

When man has thus projected his own most valuable powers onto God, what of his relationship to his own powers? They have become separated from him and in this process he has become *alienated* from himself. Everything he has is now God's and nothing is left in him. *His only access to himself is through God.* In worshiping God he tries to get in touch with that part of himself which he has lost through projection. After having given God all he has, he begs God to return to him some of what originally was his own. But having lost his own he is completely at God's mercy. He necessarily feels like a "sinner" since he has deprived himself of everything that is good, and

13. Cf. the discussion about symbiotic relationship in *Escape from Freedom,* pp. 158 ff.

it is only through God's mercy or grace that he can regain that which alone makes him human. And in order to persuade God to give him some of his love, he must prove to him how utterly deprived he is of love; in order to persuade God to guide him by his superior wisdom he must prove to him how deprived he is of wisdom when he is left to himself.

But this alienation from his own powers not only makes man feel slavishly dependent on God, it makes him bad too. He becomes a man without faith in his fellow men or in himself, without the experience of his own love, of his own power of reason. As a result the separation between the "holy" and the "secular" occurs. In his worldly activities man acts without love, in that sector of his life which is reserved to religion he feels himself to be a sinner (which he actually is, since to live without love is to live in sin) and tries to recover some of his lost humanity by being in touch with God. Simultaneously, he tries to win forgiveness by emphasizing his own helplessness and worthlessness. Thus the attempt to obtain forgiveness results in the activation of the very attitude from which his sins stem. He is caught in a painful dilemma. The more he praises God, the emptier he becomes. The emptier he becomes, the more sinful he feels. The more sinful he feels, the more he praises his God—and the less able is he to regain himself.

Analysis of religion must not stop at uncovering those psychological processes within man which underly his religious experience; it must proceed to discover the conditions which make for the development of authoritarian and humanistic character structures, respectively, from which different kinds of religious experience stem. Such a sociopsychological analysis goes far beyond the context of these chapters. However, the principal point can be made briefly. What people think and feel is rooted in their character and their character is molded by the total configuration of their practice of life—more precisely, by the socioeconomic and political structure of their society. In societies ruled by a powerful minority which holds the masses in subjection, the individual will be so imbued with fear, so incapable of feeling strong or independent, that his religious experience will be authoritarian. Whether he worships a punishing, awesome God or a similarly conceived leader makes little difference. On the other hand, where the individual feels free and responsible for his own fate, or among minorities striving for freedom and independence, humanistic religious experience develops. The history of religion gives ample evidence of this correlation between social structure and kinds of religious experience. Early Christianity was a religion of the poor and downtrodden; the history of religious sects fighting against authoritarian political pressure shows the same principle again and again. Judaism, in which a strong anti-authoritarian tradition could grow up because secular authority never had much of a chance to govern and to build up a legend of its wisdom, therefore developed the humanistic aspect of religion to a remarkable degree. Whenever, on the other hand, religion allied itself with secular power, the religion had by necessity to become authoritarian. The real fall of man is his alienation from himself, his submission to power, his turning against himself even though under the guise of his worship of God.

From the spirit of authoritarian religion stem two fallacies of reasoning which have been used again and again as arguments for theistic religion. One argument runs as follows: How can you criticize the emphasis on dependence on a power transcending man; is not man dependent on forces outside himself which he cannot understand, much less control?

Indeed, man is dependent; he remains subject to death, age, illness, and even if he were to control nature and to make it wholly serviceable to him, he and his earth remain tiny specks in the universe. But it is one thing to recognize one's dependence and limitations, and it is something entirely different to indulge in this dependence, to worship the forces on which one depends. To understand realistically and soberly how limited our power is is an essential part of wisdom and of maturity; to worship it is masochistic and self-destructive. The one is humility, the other self-humiliation.

We can study the difference between the realistic recognition of our limitations and the indulgence in the experience of submission and powerlessness in the clinical examination of masochistic character traits. We find people who have a tendency to incur sickness, accidents, humiliating situations, who belittle and weaken themselves. They believe that they get into such situations against their will and intention, but a study of their unconscious motives shows that actually they are driven by one of the most irrational tendencies to be found in man, namely, by an unconscious desire to be weak and powerless; they tend to shift the center of their life to powers over which they feel no control, thus escaping from freedom and from personal responsibility. We find furthermore that this masochistic tendency is usually accompanied by its very opposite, the tendency to rule and to dominate others, and that the masochistic and the dominating tendencies form the two sides of the authoritarian character structure.[14] Such masochistic tendencies are not always unconscious. We find them overtly in the sexual masochistic perversion where the fulfillment of the wish to be hurt or humiliated is the condition for sexual excitement and satisfaction. We find it also in the relationship to the leader and the state in all authoritarian secular religions. Here the explicit aim is to give up one's own will and to experience submission under the leader or the state as profoundly rewarding.

Another fallacy of theological thinking is closely related to the one concerning dependence. I mean here the argument that there must be a power or being outside of man because we find that man has an ineradicable longing to relate himself to something beyond himself. Indeed, any sane human being has a need to relate himself to others; a person who has lost that capacity completely is insane. No wonder that man has created figures outside of himself to

14. See *Escape from Freedom*, pp. 141 ff.

which he relates himself, which he loves and cherishes because they are not subject to the vacillations and inconsistencies of human objects. That God is a symbol of man's need to love is simple enough to understand. But does it follow from the existence and intensity of this human need that there exists an outer being who corresponds to this need? Obviously that follows as little as our strongest desire to love someone proves that there is a person with whom we are in love. All it proves is our need and perhaps our capacity.

In this chapter I have attempted to psychoanalyze various aspects of religion. I might have started it with the discussion of a more general problem, the psychoanalytic approach to thought systems, religious, philosophical, and political. But I believe that it is more helpful to the reader to consider this general problem now after the discussion of the specific issues has permitted a more concrete approach.

Among the most important findings of psychoanalysis are those concerning the validity of thoughts and ideas. Traditional theories took as their basic data in the study of man's mind his own ideas about himself. Men were supposed to start wars motivated by their concern for honor, patriotism, freedom—because they thought they did. Parents were supposed to punish children out of their sense of duty and concern for their children—because they thought they did. People were supposed to kill unbelievers prompted by the wish to please God—because they thought they did. A new attitude toward man's thought slowly made its appearance, of which the first utterance is Spinoza's statement: "What Paul says about Peter tells us more about Paul than about Peter." With this attitude, our interest in Paul's statement is not in what *he* thinks it should be, namely, in Peter; we take it as a statement about Paul. We say that we know Paul better than he knows himself; we can decipher his thoughts because we are not taken in by the fact that he intends to communicate only a statement about Peter; we listen, as Theodor Reik phrased it, with "a third ear." Spinoza's statement contains an essential point of Freud's theory of man: that a great deal of what matters goes on behind one's back, and that people's conscious ideas are only *one* datum which has no greater relevancy than any other behavior datum; in fact often less.

Does this dynamic theory of man mean that reason, thought, and consciousness are of no importance and ought to be disregarded? In an understandable reaction to the traditional overestimation of conscious thought some psychoanalysts have tended to be skeptical toward any kind of thought system, interpreting it as being nothing but the rationalization of impulses and desires rather than considering it in terms of its own logical frame of reference. They have been particularly skeptical of all kinds of religious or philosophical statements and have been prone to view them as obsessional thinking which in itself must not be taken seriously. We must call this attitude an error not only from a philosophical standpoint but from the standpoint of psychoanalysis itself, because psychoanalysis while debunking rationalizations has made reason the tool with which we achieve such critical analyses of rationalization.

Psychoanalysis has demonstrated the ambiguous nature of our thinking processes. Indeed, the power of rationalization, this counterfeit of reason, is one of the most puzzling human phenomena. If we were not so accustomed to it, man's rationalizing effort would clearly appear to us as similar to a paranoid system. The paranoid person can be very intelligent, make excellent use of his reason in all areas of life except in that isolated part where his paranoid system is involved. The rationalizing person does exactly the same. We talk to an intelligent Stalinist who exhibits a great capacity to make use of his reason in many areas of thought. When we come to discuss Stalinism with him, however, we are suddenly confronted with a closed system of thought, the only function of which is to prove that his allegiance to Stalinism is in line with and not contradictory to reason. He will deny certain obvious facts, distort others, or, inasmuch as he agrees to certain facts and statements, he will explain his attitude as logical and consistent. He will at the same time declare that the fascist cult of the leader is one of the most obnoxious features of authoritarianism and claim that the Stalinist cult of the leader is something entirely different, that it is the genuine expression of the people's love for Stalin. When you tell him that is what the Nazis claimed too, he will smile tolerantly about your want of perception or accuse you of being the lackey of capitalism. He will find a thousand and one reasons why Russian nationalism is not nationalism, why authoritarianism is democracy, why slave labor is designed to educate and improve antisocial elements. The arguments which are used to defend or explain the deeds of the inquisition or those used to explain racial or sex prejudices are illustrations of the same rationalizing capacity.

The degree to which man uses his thinking to rationalize irrational passions and to justify the actions of his group shows how great the distance is which man has still to travel in order to become Homo sapiens. But we must go beyond such an awareness. We must try to understand the reasons for this phenomenon lest we fall into the error of believing that man's readiness for rationalization is a part of "human nature" which nothing can change.

Man by origin is a herd animal. His actions are determined by an instinctive impulse to follow the leader and to have close contact with the other animals around him. Inasmuch as we are sheep, there is no greater threat to our existence than to lose this contact with the herd and to be isolated. Right and wrong, true and false are determined by the herd. But we are not only sheep. We are also human; we are endowed with awareness of ourselves, endowed with reason which by its very nature is independent of the herd. Our actions can be determined by the results of our thinking regardless of whether or not the truth is shared by others.

The split between our sheep nature and our human

nature is the basis for two kinds of orientations: *the orientation by proximity to the herd and the orientation by reason.* Rationalization is a compromise between our sheep nature and our human capacity to think. The latter forces us to make believe that everything we do can stand the test of reason, and that is why we tend to make it appear that our irrational opinions and decisions are reasonable. But inasmuch as we are sheep, reason is not our real guide; we are guided by an entirely different principle, that of herd allegiance.

The ambiguity of thinking, the dichotomy between reason and a rationalizing intellect, is the expression of a basic dichotomy in man, the coextensive need for bondage and freedom. The unfolding and full emergence of reason is dependent on the attainment of full freedom and independence. Until this is accomplished man will tend to accept for truth that which the majority of his group want to be true; his judgment is determined by need for contact with the herd and by fear of being isolated from it. A few individuals can stand this isolation and say the truth in spite of the danger of losing touch. They are the true heroes of the human race but for whom we should still be living in caves. Yet for the vast majority of men who are not heroes the development of reason depends on the emergence of a social order in which each individual is fully respected and not made a tool by the state or by any other group, a social order in which he need not be afraid to criticize and in which the pursuit of truth does not isolate man from his brothers but makes him feel one with them. It follows that man will attain the full capacity for objectivity and reason only when a society of man is established above all particular divisions of the human race, when loyalty to the human race and to its ideals is considered the prime loyalty that exists.

The minute study of the process of rationalization is perhaps the most significant contribution of psychoanalysis to human progress. It has opened up a new dimension of the truth, it has shown that the fact that someone sincerely believes in a statement is not enough to determine his sincerity, that only by understanding the unconscious processes going on in him can we know whether he rationalizes or whether he speaks the truth.[15]

Psychoanalysis of thought processes is not only concerned with those rationalizing thoughts which tend to distort or hide the true motivation but also with such thoughts which are untrue in another sense, that of not having the weight and significance which is attributed to them by those who profess them. A thought may be an empty shell, nothing but an

15. One misunderstanding which easily arises at this point must be dispelled. The truth in the sense in which we speak of it here refers to the question of whether a motive given by a person as reason for his action is the true motivation as far as he is concerned. It does not refer to the truth of the rationalizing statement as such. To give a simple example: if someone who is afraid of meeting a certain person gives as the reason why he does not want to see him that it is raining heavily, he is rationalizing. The true reason is his fear and not the rain. The rationalizing statement, namely, that it is raining, may in itself be a true statement.

opinion held because it is the thought pattern of the culture which one adopts easily and could shed easily provided public opinion changes. A thought, on the other hand, may be the expression of the person's feelings and genuine convictions. In the latter case it is rooted in his total personality and has an *emotional matrix*. Only those thoughts which are thus rooted determine effectively the person's action.

A recent survey [16] offers a good illustration. Two questions were asked of whites in the North and South of the United States: (1) Are all men created equal? (2) Are the Negroes equal to the whites? Even in the South 61 per cent answered the first question in the affirmative but only 4 per cent answered the second question in the affirmative. (For the North the figures were 79 per cent and 21 per cent, respectively.) The person who assented only to the first question undoubtedly remembered it as a thought learned in classes and retained because it is still part of a generally recognized, respectable ideology, but it has no relation to what the person really feels; it is, as it were, in his head, without any connection with his heart and hence without any power to influence his action. The same holds true for any number of respectable ideas. A survey today in the United States would show almost complete unanimity that democracy is the best form of government. But this result does not prove that all those who expressed an opinion in favor of democracy would fight for it if it were

16. *Negro Digest,* 1945.

threatened; even most of those who in their hearts are authoritarian personalities would express democratic opinions as long as the majority does so.

Any idea is strong only if it is grounded in a person's character structure. No idea is more potent than its emotional matrix. The psychoanalytic approach to religion then aims at the *understanding of human reality behind thought systems*. It inquires whether a thought system is expressive of the feeling which it portrays or whether it is a rationalization hiding opposite attitudes. Furthermore it asks whether the thought system grows from a strong emotional matrix or whether it is an empty opinion.

While it is relatively easy to describe the principle of this approach, the analysis of any thought system is exceedingly difficult. The analyst in trying to determine the human reality behind a thought system must in the first place consider the system as a whole. The meaning of any single part of a philosophical or religious system can be determined only within the whole context of that system. Should a part become isolated from its context the door is open to any kind of arbitrary misinterpretation. In the process of scrutinizing a system as a whole it is particularly important to watch any inconsistencies or contradictions within the system; these usually will point to discrepancies between consciously held opinion and underlying feeling. Calvin's views on predestination, for instance, which claim that the decision whether a man is to be saved or sentenced to eternal damnation is made before he is born and without his possessing

the ability to change his own fate are in blatant contradiction to the idea of God's love. The psychoanalyst must study the personality and character
structure of those who profess certain thought systems, both as individuals and as groups. He will in-
quire into the consistencies of character structure
with professed opinion and will interpret the thought
system in terms of the unconscious forces which can
be inferred from minute details of manifest behavior.
He finds, for instance, that the way a man looks at
his neighbor or talks to a child, the way he eats, walks,
or shakes hands, or the way in which a group behaves
toward minorities is more expressive of faith and
love then any stated belief. From the study of thought
systems in connection with the character structure he
will attempt to find an answer to the question whether
and to what extent the thought system is a rationalization and how great the weight of the thought system is.

If the psychoanalyst is primarily interested in the
human reality behind religious doctrines, he will find
the same reality underlying different religions and
opposite human attitudes underlying the same religion. The human reality, for instance, underlying
the teachings of Buddha, Isaiah, Christ, Socrates, or
Spinoza is essentially the same. It is determined by
the striving for love, truth, and justice. The human
reality behind Calvin's theological system and that of
authoritarian political systems is also very similar.
Their spirit is one of submission to power and lack of
love and of respect for the individual.

Just as a parent's consciously felt or expressed concern for a child can be an expression of love or can express a wish for control and domination, a religious statement can be expressive of opposite human attitudes. We do not discard that statement but look at it in perspective, the human reality behind it providing the third dimension. Particularly concerning the sincerity of the postulate of love the words hold true: "By their fruits shall ye know them." If religious teachings contribute to the growth, strength, freedom, and happiness of their believers, we see the fruits of love. If they contribute to the constriction of human potentialities, to unhappiness and lack of productivity, they cannot be born of love, regardless of what the dogma intends to convey.

IV

THE PSYCHOANALYST AS "PHYSICIAN OF THE SOUL"

THERE are today various schools of psycho-analysis ranging from the more or less strict adherents to Freud's theory to the "revisionists" who differ among themselves in the degree to which they have changed Freud's concepts.[1] For our purpose, however, these differences are much less important than the difference between that psychoanalysis which aims primarily at *social adjustment* and psycho-analysis which aims at the "*cure of the soul.*"[2]

In the beginning of its development psychoanalysis was a branch of medicine and its aim was to cure sickness. The patients coming to the psychoanalyst suffered from symptoms which interfered with their functioning in everyday life; such symptoms were expressed in ritualistic compulsions, obsessional thoughts, phobias, paranoid thought systems, and so on. The only difference between these patients and those who went to a regular physician was that the causes of their symptoms were to be found not in the body but in the psyche, and the therapy was there-

1. Cf. Clara Thompson, with the collaboration of Patrick Mullahy, *Psychoanalysis: Evolution and Development* (Hermitage House, Inc., 1950); and Patrick Mullahy, *Oedipus—Myth and Complex* (Hermitage House, Inc., 1948).

2. Let us remember here that "cure" has not the single connotation of remedial treatment which modern usage commonly implies, but is used in its larger sense of "caring for."

fore concerned not with somatic but with psychic phenomena. But the aim of the psychoanalytic therapy was not different from the therapeutic aim in medicine: the removal of the symptom. If the patient was freed from psychogenic vomiting or coughing, from his compulsive acts or obsessive thoughts, he was considered cured.

In the course of his work Freud and his collaborators became increasingly aware that the symptom was only the most conspicuous and, as it were, dramatic expression of the neurotic disturbance, and that in order to achieve lasting and not merely symptomatic relief one must analyze the person's character and help the patient in the process of character reorientation. This development was furthered by a new trend among patients. Many people who came to psychoanalysts were not sick in the traditional sense of the word and had none of the overt symptoms mentioned above. They were not insane either. They often were not considered sick by their relatives and friends, and yet they suffered from "difficulties in living"—to use Harry Stack Sullivan's formulation of the psychiatric problem—which led them to seek help from a psychoanalyst. Such difficulties in living were of course nothing new. There have always been people who feel insecure or inferior, who cannot find happiness in their marriages, who have difficulties in accomplishing or enjoying their work, who are inordinately afraid of other people, and so on. They might have sought help from a priest, a friend, a philosopher—or "just lived" with their troubles without asking for help of any specific kind. What was new was the fact that Freud and his school offered for the first time a comprehensive theory of character, an explanation for the difficulties in living in so far as these are rooted in the character structure, and a hope for change. Thus, psychoanalysis shifted its emphasis more and more from therapy of the neurotic *symptoms* to therapy of difficulties in living rooted in the neurotic *character*.

While it is relatively simple to decide what the therapeutic aim is in cases of hysterical vomiting or of obsessional thinking, it is not equally simple to decide what the therapeutic aim should be in a case of a character neurosis; in fact, it is not even simple to say what the patient suffers from.

The following case should explain what is meant by this statement.[3] A young man of twenty-four comes to see an analyst; he reports that since his graduation from college two years ago he has felt miserable. He works in his father's firm but does not enjoy the work, is moody, has frequent sharp conflicts with his father; furthermore, he has difficulties in making even the smallest decisions. He says that all this started a few months before his graduation from college. He was very interested in physics; his teacher had told him that he had considerable gifts for theoretical physics and he had wanted to go to graduate school and find his life's work as a scientist. His father, a well-to-do

3. This, like all other clinical illustrations in this book, is not drawn from my own patients but from case material presented by students. Details are changed so as to make any identification impossible.

businessman, owner of a large factory, insisted that the son should enter his business, take the burden from his shoulders, and eventually become his successor. He argued that he had no other children, he had built up the firm all by himself, the doctor had advised him to work less strenuously, and the son would be ungrateful if, under these circumstances, he were unwilling to fulfill his father's wish. The son, as the result of his father's promises, warnings, and appeals to his sense of loyalty, had given in and entered his father's firm. Then the troubles described above began.

What in this case is the problem and what is the cure? There are two ways of looking at the situation. One can argue that the father's standpoint is perfectly reasonable; that the son would have followed the father's advice without much trouble were it not for an irrational rebelliousness, a deeply buried antagonism to his father; that his wish to become a physicist is not so much based on his interest in physics as on his antagonism to his father and the unconscious wish to frustrate him. While he has followed his father's advice, he has not stopped fighting him; in fact, his antagonism has even grown since his giving in. His difficulties stem from this unresolved antagonism. If it were resolved by digging into its deeper causes, the son would have no difficulty making reasonable decisions, and his worries, doubts, and so forth would disappear.

If one looks at the situation differently, the argument runs something like this. While the father may have every reason to wish that his son join his firm and while he has the right to express his wishes, the son has the right—and morally speaking the obligation—to do what his conscience and his sense of integrity tell him. If he feels that life as a physicist is most adequate to his gifts and desires, he must follow this calling rather than his father's wishes. There is indeed some antagonism to the father, not an irrational antagonism based on imaginary reasons which would disappear when analyzed but a rational antagonism which was formed as a reaction against the father's authoritarian-possessive attitude. If we look at the patient's difficulties from this viewpoint the trouble and the therapeutic aim are quite different from what they appear to be in the first interpretation. The symptom now is the inability to assert himself sufficiently and fear of following his own plans and desires. He is cured when he is no longer afraid of his father; and the aim of therapy is to help him attain courage to assert and to emancipate himself. In this view one would discover a good deal of repressed hostility against the father, but this hostility would be understood not as the cause but as a result of the basic trouble. Obviously, either interpretation can be true, and from one's knowledge of all the details of the patient's and his father's characters one must decide which one is correct in a given case. But the analyst's judgment will also be influenced by his philosophy and his system of values. If one is prone to believe that "adjustment" to the social patterns is the paramount aim of life, that practical considera-

tions like the continuity of a firm, higher income, gratitude toward parents are prime considerations, one
will also be more inclined to interpret the son's trouble
in terms of his irrational antagonism to the father.
If, on the other hand, one considers integrity, independence, and the doing of work meaningful to the
person as supreme values, one will be prone to look
at the son's inability to assert himself and his fear of
his father as the main difficulties to be resolved.

Another case illustrates the same point. A gifted
writer comes to an analyst with complaints of headaches and spells of dizziness for which, according to
his physician's statement, there is no organic basis.
He tells the story of his life up to the present. Two
years ago he accepted a job which was highly desirable
as far as income, security, and prestige were concerned. In a conventional sense getting this job
amounted to a tremendous success. On the other hand,
it has obliged him to write things which run counter
to his convictions and in which he does not believe.
He has spent a great deal of energy trying to square
his actions with his conscience, making a number of
complicated constructions to prove that his intellectual and moral integrity are not really touched by the
kind of work he is doing. Headaches and feelings of
dizziness began to appear. It is not very difficult to
discover that these symptoms are an expression of the
unresolved conflict between his wish for money and
prestige on the one hand and his moral scruples on
the other. But if we ask what is the pathological, neurotic element in this conflict, two psychoanalysts may

look at the situation in different ways. It can be argued that to have taken the job was a perfectly normal step, that it was a sign of healthy adjustment to our culture, and that the decision the writer made is the one any normal, well-adjusted person would have made. The neurotic element in the situation is his inability to accept his own decision. It may be that we find here a repetition of old guilt feelings which belong to his childhood, guilt feelings related to the Oedipus complex, masturbation, stealing, and so on. There may also be a self-punishing tendency in him which makes him feel badly precisely when he has attained success. If one takes this viewpoint the therapeutic problem is his inability to accept his own reasonable decision, and he would be cured if he were to lose his scruples and become satisfied with his present situation.

Another analyst may look at the situation in exactly the opposite way. He will start out with the assumption that intellectual and moral integrity cannot be violated without damage to the whole personality. The fact that the patient follows a culturally approved pattern does not alter this basic principle. The difference between this man and many others is only that the voice of his conscience is sufficiently alive to cause an acute conflict where others might not become aware of this conflict and would not have such manifest symptoms. The problem from this viewpoint would appear to be the writer's difficulty in following the voice of his conscience, and he would be considered cured if he could rid himself of his present situation and resume a life in which he could respect himself.

Still another case throws light on the problem from a slightly different angle. A businessman, intelligent, aggressive, successful, has come to drink more and more heavily. He turns to a psychoanalyst to be cured of his drinking. His life is completely devoted to competition and money making. Nothing else interests him; his personal relationships all serve the same goal. He is expert in making friends and gaining influence, but deep down he hates everyone he comes in contact with, his competitors, his customers, his employees. He also hates the commodity he sells. He has no particular interest in it except as a means to make money. He is not conscious of this hate, but slowly one can recognize from his dreams and free associations that he feels like a slave to his business, his commodity, and everyone connected with it; he has no respect for himself and dulls the pain of feeling inferior and worthless by resorting to drinking. He has never been in love with anyone and satisfies his sexual desires in cheap and meaningless affairs.

What is his problem? Is it his drinking? Or is his drinking only a symptom of his real problem, his failure to lead a meaningful life? Can a man live with this degree of alienation from himself, with so much hate and so little love, without feeling inferior and without being disturbed? Undoubtedly there are many people who can do so without symptoms and without becoming aware of any disturbance. Their problems begin when they are not busy, when they are alone. But they succeed in using any number of the avenues of escape from the self which our culture offers to silence any manifestation of their dissatisfaction. Those who develop an overt symptom show that their human powers are not completely stifled. Something in them protests and thus indicates conflict. They are not sicker than those whose adjustment has been completely successful. On the contrary, in a human sense they are healthier. From this latter standpoint we do not look at the symptom as an enemy to be defeated, but on the contrary as the friend that points out to us that something is wrong. The patient, however unconsciously, is striving for a more humane way of living. His problem is not his drinking but his moral failure. His cure cannot be effected in terms of his manifest symptom. If he were to stop drinking without changing anything else in his scheme of life he would remain uneasy and tense, he would be forced into more and more active competitiveness, and probably at one time or another would develop another symptom expressive of his dissatisfaction. What he needs is someone who can help him uncover the reasons for this waste of his best human powers and thus regain their use.

We see that it is not easy to determine what we consider to be the sickness and what we consider to be the cure. The solution depends on what one considers to be the aim of psychoanalysis. We find that according to one conception *adjustment* is the aim of analytic cure. By adjustment is meant a person's ability to act like the majority of people in his culture. In this view those existing patterns of behavior which society and the culture approve provide the criteria for mental health. These criteria are not critically examined from the standpoint of universal human norms but rather express a social relativism which takes this "rightness" for granted and considers behavior deviant from them to be wrong, hence unhealthy. Therapy aiming at nothing but social adjustment can only reduce the excessive suffering of the neurotic to the average level of suffering inherent in conformity to these patterns.

In the second view the aim of therapy is not primarily adjustment but optimal development of a person's potentialities and the realization of his individuality. Here the psychoanalyst is not an "adjustment counselor" but, to use Plato's expression, the "physician of the soul." This view is based on the premise that there are immutable laws inherent in human nature and human functioning which operate in any given culture. These laws cannot be violated without serious damage to the personality. If someone violates his moral and intellectual integrity he weakens or even paralyzes his total personality. He is unhappy and suffers. If his way of living is approved by his culture the suffering may not be conscious or it may be felt as being related to things entirely separate from his real problem. But in spite of what he thinks, the problem of mental health cannot be separated from the basic human problem, that of achieving the aims of human life: independence, integrity, and the ability to love.

In making this distinction between adjustment and the cure of the soul I have described *principles* of therapy but I do not intend to imply that one can make such a clear-cut distinction in practice. There are many kinds of psychoanalytic procedure in which both principles are blended; sometimes the emphasis is on one, sometimes on the other. But it is important to recognize the distinction between these principles because only then can we recognize their respective weight in any given analysis. Nor do I wish to give the impression that one must chose between social adjustment and concern with one's soul, and that chosing the path of human integrity necessarily leads one into the desert of social failure.

The "adjusted" person in the sense in which I have used the term here is one who has made himself into a commodity, with nothing stable or definite except his need to please and his readiness to change roles. As long as he succeeds in his efforts he enjoys a certain amount of security, but his betrayal of the higher self, of human values, leaves an inner emptiness and insecurity which will become manifest when anything goes wrong in his battle for success. And even if nothing should go wrong he often pays for his human failure with ulcers, heart trouble, or any of the other psychically determined kinds of illness. The person who has attained inner strength and integrity often may not be as successful as his unscrupulous neighbor but he will have security, judgment, and objectivity which will make him much less vulnerable to changing fortunes and opinions of others and will in many areas enhance his ability for constructive work.

It is obvious that "adjustment therapy" can have

no religious function, provided that by religious we refer to the attitude common to the original teachings of humanistic religions. I wish now to show that psychoanalysis as a cure of the soul has very definitely a religious function in this sense, although it will usually lead to a more critical attitude toward theistic dogma.

In trying to give a picture of the human attitude underlying the thinking of Lao-tse, Buddha, the Prophets, Socrates, Jesus, Spinoza, and the philosophers of the Enlightenment, one is struck by the fact that in spite of significant differences there is a core of ideas and norms common to all of these teachings. Without attempting to arrive at a complete and precise formulation, the following is an approximate description of this common core: man must strive to recognize the truth and can be fully human only to the extent to which he succeeds in this task. He must be independent and free, an end in himself and not the means for any other person's purposes. He must relate himself to his fellow men lovingly. If he has no love, he is an empty shell even if his were all power, wealth, and intelligence. Man must know the difference between good and evil, he must learn to listen to the voice of his conscience and to be able to follow it.

The following remarks attempt to show that the aim of the psychoanalytic cure of the soul is to help the patient attain the attitude which I just described as religious.

In our discussion of Freud I have indicated that to

recognize the *truth* is a basic aim of the psychoanalytic process. Psychoanalysis has given the concept of truth a new dimension. In pre-analytic thinking a person could be considered to speak the truth if he believed in what he was saying. Psychoanalysis has shown that subjective conviction is by no means a sufficient criterion of sincerity. A person can believe that he acts out of a sense of justice and yet be motivated by cruelty. He can believe that he is motivated by love and yet be driven by a craving for masochistic dependence. A person can believe that duty is his guide though his main motivation is vanity. In fact most rationalizations are held to be true by the person who uses them. He not only wants others to believe his rationalizations but believes them himself, and the more he wants to protect himself from recognizing his true motivation the more ardently he must believe in them. Furthermore, in the psychoanalytic process a person learns to recognize which of his ideas have an emotional matrix and which are only conventional clichés without root in his character structure and therefore without substance and weight. The psychoanalytic process is in itself a search for truth. The object of this search is the truth about phenomena not outside of man but in man himself. It is based on the principle that mental health and happiness cannot be achieved unless we scrutinize our thinking and feeling to detect whether we rationalize and whether our beliefs are rooted in our feeling.

The idea that critical self-evaluation and the resulting ability to discern between genuine and false experience are essential elements in a religious attitude is beautifully expressed in an old religious document of Buddhist origin. We find in the Tibetan Precepts of the Gurus an enumeration of the ten resemblances in which one may err:

"1. Desire may be mistaken for faith.

2. Attachment may be mistaken for benevolence and compassion.

3. Cessation of thought-processes may be mistaken for the quiescence of infinite mind, which is the true goal.

4. Sense perceptions (or phenomena) may be mistaken for revelations (or glimpses) of Reality.

5. A mere glimpse of Reality may be mistaken for complete realization.

6. Those who outwardly profess, but do not practice religion may be mistaken for true devotees.

7. Slaves of passion may be mistaken for masters of Yoga who have liberated themselves from all conventional laws.

8. Actions performed in the interest of self may be mistakenly regarded as being altruistic.

9. Deceptive methods may be mistakenly regarded as being prudent.

10. Charlatans may be mistaken for Sages." [4]

Indeed, to help man discern truth from falsehood in himself is the basic aim of psychoanalysis, a thera-

4. *Tibetan Yoga and Secret Doctrines,* W. Y. Evans-Wentz, ed. (Oxford University Press, 1935), p. 77. Quoted by Frederic Spiegelberg, *The Religion of No-Religion* (James Ladd Delkin, 1948), p. 52.

peutic method which is an empirical application of the statement, "The truth shall make you free."

Both in humanistic religious thinking and in psychoanalysis man's ability to search for the truth is held to be inseparably linked to the attainment of *freedom* and *independence*.

Freud states that the Oedipus complex is the core of every neurosis. His assumption is that the child is bound to the parent of the opposite sex and that mental illness results if the child does not overcome this infantile fixation. For Freud the assumption that incestuous impulses must be a deeply rooted human passion seemed inescapable. He gained this impression from the study of clinical material, but the ubiquity of incest tabus was to him an additional proof of his thesis. As is often the case, however, the full significance of Freud's discovery can be recognized only if we translate it from the sphere of sex into that of interpersonal relations. The essence of incest is not the sexual craving for members of the same family. This craving, in so far as it is to be found, is only one expression of the much more profound and fundamental desire to remain a child attached to those protecting figures of whom the mother is the earliest and most influential. The foetus lives with and from the mother, and the act of birth is only one step in the direction of freedom and independence. The infant after birth is still in many ways part and parcel of the mother, and its birth as an independent person is a process which takes many years—which, in fact, takes a whole life. To cut through the navel string, not in the physical but in the psychological sense, is the great challenge to human development and also its most difficult task. As long as man is related by these primary ties to mother, father, family, he feels protected and safe. He is still a foetus, someone else is responsible for him. He avoids the disquieting experience of seeing himself as a separate entity charged with the responsibility for his own actions, with the task of making his own judgments, "of taking his life in his hands." By remaining a child man not only avoids the fundamental anxiety necessarily connected with the full awareness of one's self as a separate entity, he also enjoys the satisfactions of protection, warmth, and of unquestioned belonging which he once enjoyed as a child; but he pays a high price. He fails to become a full human being, to develop his powers of reason and of love; he remains dependent and retains a feeling of insecurity which becomes manifest at any moment when these primary ties are threatened. All his mental and emotional activities are geared to the authority of his primary group; hence his beliefs and insights are not his own. He can feel affection but it is animal affection, the warmth of the stable, and not human love which has freedom and separateness as its condition. The incestuously orientated person is capable of feeling close to those whom he is familiar with. He is incapable of relating himself closely to the "stranger," that is, to another human being as such. In this orientation all feelings and ideas are judged in terms not of good and evil or true and false but of familiar and unfamiliar. When Jesus said, "For I am come to set a man at variance against his father, and the daughter against her mother, and the daughter in law against her mother in law," [5] he did not mean to teach hatred of parents but to express in the most unequivocal and drastic form the principle that man must break incestuous ties and become free in order to become human.

The attachment to parents is only one, though the most fundamental, form of incest; in the process of social evolution other attachments in part replace it. The tribe, the nation, the race, the state, the social class, political parties, and many other forms of institutions and organizations become home and family. Here are the roots of nationalism and racism, which in turn are symptoms of man's inability to experience himself and others as free human beings. It may be said that the development of mankind is the development from incest to freedom. In this lies the explanation for the universality of incest tabus. The human race could not have progressed had it not guided the need for closeness into channels away from mother, father, and siblings. Love for a wife is dependent on overcoming the incestuous strivings; "therefore shall a man leave his father and his mother and shall cleave unto his wife." But the significance of the tabu on incest goes far beyond this. The growth of

5. Matthew 10:35.

reason and of all rational value judgments requires that man overcome the incestuous fixation with its criteria of right and wrong based on familiarity.

The integration of small groups into larger ones, and its biological consequences, would have been impossible without incest tabus. No wonder that an aim so imperative from the standpoint of social evolution has been safeguarded by forceful and universal tabus. But while we have traveled a long road toward overcoming incest, mankind has by no means succeeded in its conquest. The groupings to which man feels incestuously tied have become larger and the area of freedom has become greater, but the ties to those larger units which substitute for the clan and the soil are still powerful and strong. Only the complete eradication of incestuous fixation will permit the realization of the brotherhood of man.

To sum up, Freud's statement that the Oedipus complex, the incestuous fixation, is the "kernel of neurosis" is one of the most significant insights into the problem of mental health when we free it from its narrow formulation in sexual terms and understand it in its broad interpersonal significance. Freud himself has indicated that he means something beyond the sexual realm.[6] In fact, his view that man must leave father and mother and grow up to face reality constitutes his main argument against religion in *The Future of an Illusion,* wherein his criticism of religion is that it keeps man in bondage and depend-

6. Jung has pointed out the necessity of such revision of Freud's incest concepts clearly and convincingly in his early writings.

ence and thus prevents him from attaining the paramount task of human existence, that of freedom and independence.

It would of course be a mistake to assume that the foregoing remarks imply that only those who are "neurotic" have failed in this task of self-emancipation, while the average well-adjusted person has succeeded in it. On the contrary, the vast majority of people in our culture are well adjusted because they have given up the battle for independence sooner and more radically than the neurotic person. They have accepted the judgment of the majority so completely that they have been spared the sharp pain of conflict which the neurotic person goes through. While they are healthy from the standpoint of "adjustment," they are more sick than the neurotic person from the standpoint of the realization of their aims as human beings. Can theirs then be a perfect solution? It would be if it were possible to ignore the fundamental laws of human existence without damage. But that is not possible. The "adjusted" person who does not live by the truth and who does not love is protected only from manifest conflicts. If he is not engrossed in work he has to use the many avenues of escape which our culture offers in order to be protected from the frightening experience of being alone with himself and looking into the abyss of his own impotence and human impoverishment.

All great religions have proceeded from the negative formulation of incest tabus to more positive formulations of freedom. Buddha had his insights in solitude. He makes the extreme demand that man rid himself of all "familiar" ties in order to find himself and his real strength. The Jewish-Christian religion is not as radical as Buddhism in this respect but it is not less clear. In the myth of the Garden of Eden man's existence is described as one of complete security. He is lacking in knowledge of good and evil. Human history begins with man's act of disobedience which is at the same time the beginning of his freedom and the development of his reason. The Jewish and particularly the Christian traditions have stressed the element of sin but have ignored the fact that it is the emancipation from the security of Paradise which is the basis for man's truly human development. The demand to sever the ties of blood and soil runs through the entire Old Testament. Abraham is told to leave his country and become a wanderer. Moses is brought up as a stranger in an unfamiliar environment away from his family and even from his own people. The condition for Israel's mission as God's chosen people lies in their leaving the bondage of Egypt and wandering in the desert for forty years. After having settled down in their own country, they fall back into the incestuous worship of the soil, of idols, and of the state. The central issue of the teachings of the Prophets is the fight against this incestuous worship. They preach instead the basic values common to all mankind, those of truth, love, and justice. They attack the state and those secular powers which fail to realize these norms. The state must perish if man becomes tied to it in such a way that the welfare of the state, its power and its glory become the criteria of good and evil. The concept that the people must go into exile again and can return to their soil only when they have achieved freedom and ceased the idolatrous worship of soil and state is the logical culmination of this principle which underlies the Old Testament and particularly the messianic concept of the Prophets.

Only if one has outgrown incestuous ties can one judge one's own group critically; only then can one judge at all. Most groups, whether they are primitive tribes, nations, or religions, are concerned with their own survival and upholding the power of their leaders, and they exploit the inherent moral sense of their members to arouse them against outsiders with whom there is conflict. But they use the incestuous ties which keep a person in moral bondage to his own group to stifle his moral sense and his judgment, so that he will not criticize his own group for violations of moral principles which if committed by others would drive him into violent opposition.

It is the tragedy of all great religions that they violate and pervert the very principles of freedom as soon as they become mass organizations governed by a religious bureaucracy. The religious organization and the men who represent it take over to some extent the place of family, tribe, and state. They keep man in bondage instead of leaving him free. It is no longer God who is worshiped but the group that claims to speak in his name. This has happened in all religions. Their founders guided man through the desert, away from the bondage of Egypt, while later on others have led him back toward a new Egypt though calling it the Promised Land.

The command to "Love thy neighbor as thyself" is, with only slight variations in its expression, the basic principle common to all humanistic religions. But it would indeed be difficult to understand why the great spiritual teachers of the human race have *demanded* of man that he should love if love were as easy an accomplishment as most people seem to feel. What is called love? Dependence, submission, and the inability to move away from the familiar "stable," domination, possessiveness, and the craving for control are felt to be love; sexual greed and the inability to stand solitude are experienced as proof of intense capacity for love. People believe that *to love* is simple but that *to be loved* is most difficult. In our marketing orientation people think they are not loved because they are not "attractive" enough, attractiveness being based on anything from looks, dress, intelligence, money, to social position and prestige. They do not know that the real problem is not the difficulty of being loved but the difficulty of loving; that one is loved only if one can love, if one's capacity to love produces love in another person, that the capacity for love, not for its counterfeit, is a most difficult achievement.

There is hardly any situation in which the phenomenon of love and of its many distortions can be studied as intimately and accurately as in the analytic interview. There is no more convincing proof that the injunction "Love thy neighbor as thyself" is the most important norm of living and that its violation is the basic cause of unhappiness and mental illness than the evidence gathered by the psychoanalyst. Whatever complaints the neurotic patient may have, whatever symptoms he may present are rooted in his inability to love, if we mean by love a capacity for the experience of concern, responsibility, respect, and understanding of another person and the intense desire for that other person's growth. *Analytic therapy is essentially an attempt to help the patient gain or regain his capacity for love.* If this aim is not fulfilled nothing but surface changes can be accomplished.

Psychoanalysis also shows that love by its very nature cannot be restricted to one person. Anyone who loves only one person and does not love "his neighbor" demonstrates that his love for one person is an attachment of submission or of domination but not love. Furthermore, anyone who loves his neighbor but does not love himself shows that the love of his neighbor is not genuine. Love is based on an attitude of affirmation and respect, and if this attitude does not also exist toward oneself, who is after all only another human being and another neighbor, it does not exist at all. The human reality behind the concept of man's love for God in humanistic religion is man's ability to love productively, to love without greed, without submission and domination, to love from the fullness of his personality, just as God's love is a symbol for love out of strength and not out of weakness.

The existence of norms which postulate how man

ought to live implies the concept of violation of these
norms, the concept of *sin* and *guilt*. There is no religion which does not deal in some fashion with sin
and with methods for recognizing and overcoming it.
The various concepts of sin differ of course with
various types of religion. In primitive religions sin
may be conceived essentially as the violation of a tabu
and of little or no ethical implication. In authoritarian
religion sin is primarily disobedience to authority
and only secondarily a violation of ethical norms. In
humanistic religion conscience is not the internalized
voice of authority but man's own voice, the guardian
of our integrity which recalls us to ourselves when we
are in danger of losing ourselves. Sin is not primarily
sin against God but sin against ourselves.[7]

The reaction to sin depends on the particular concept and experience of sin. In the authoritarian attitude the recognition of one's sins is frightening
because to have sinned means to have disobeyed
powerful authorities who will punish the sinner.
Moral failures are so many acts of rebellion which
can be atoned only in a new orgy of submission. The
reaction to one's feeling of guilt is that of being de-
praved and powerless, of throwing oneself completely
at the mercy of the authority and thus hoping to be
forgiven. The mood of this kind of contrition is one
of fear and trembling.

The result of this contrition is that the sinner, having indulged in the feeling of depravity, is morally

7. Cf. the discussion of authoritarian versus humanistic conscience in *Man for Himself,* pp. 141 ff.

weakened, filled with hate and disgust for himself, and hence prone to sin again when he is over his orgy of self-flagellation. This reaction is less extreme when his religion offers him ritualistic atonement or the words of a priest who can absolve him from his guilt. But he pays for this alleviation of the pain of guilt by dependence on those who are privileged to dispense absolution.

In the humanistic trends in religions we find an entirely different reaction to sin. Lacking the spirit of hate and intolerance, which as compensation for submission is always present in authoritarian systems, man's tendency to violate the norms for living is looked upon with understanding and love, not with scorn and contempt. The reaction to the awareness of guilt is not self-hate but an active stimulation to do better. Some Christian and Jewish mystics have even considered sin a prerequisite for the achievement of virtue. They teach that only if we sin and react to the sin not in fear but with concern for our salvation can we become fully human. In their thinking, which is centered around an affirmation of man's strength, of his likeness to God, of the experience of joy rather than that of sadness, the awareness of sins means to recognize the totality of one's own powers and is not an experience of powerlessness.

Two statements will serve to illustrate this humanistic attitude toward sin. One is Jesus' saying, "He that is without sin among you, let him first cast a stone . . ." (St. John 8: 7.) The other is a statement characteristic of mystical thinking: "Whoever talks about and reflects upon an evil thing he has done, is thinking the vileness he has perpetrated, and what one thinks, therein is one caught—with one's whole soul one is caught utterly in what one thinks, and so he is still caught in vileness. And he will surely not be able to turn, for his spirit will coarsen and his heart rot, and besides this, a sad mood may come upon him. What would you? Stir filth this way or that, and it is still filth. To have sinned or not to have sinned— what does it profit us in heaven? In the time I am brooding on this, I could be stringing pearls for the joy of heaven. That is why it is written: 'Depart from evil, and do good'—turn wholly from evil, do not brood in its way, and do good. You have done wrong? Then balance it by doing right." [8]

The problem of guilt plays no less a role in psychoanalytic procedure than it does in religion. Sometimes it is presented by the patient as one of his main symptoms. He feels guilty for not loving his parents as he should, for failing to do his work satisfactorily, for having hurt somebody's feelings. The feeling of guilt has overpowered some patients' minds and they react with a sense of inferiority, of depravity, and often with a conscious or unconscious desire for punishment. It is usually not difficult to discover that this all-pervasive guilt reaction stems from an authoritarian orientation. They would give a more correct expression to their feeling if instead of saying that they feel guilty they said that they are afraid—

8. Isaac Meir of Ger, quoted in *Time and Eternity*, N. N. Glatzer, ed. (Schocken Books, 1946), p. 111.

afraid of punishment or, more often, of not being loved any more by those authorities whom they have disobeyed. In the analytic process such a patient will slowly recognize that behind his authoritarian sense of guilt is another feeling of guilt which stems from his own voice, from his conscience in the humanistic sense. Assume that a patient feels guilty for leading a promiscuous life. The first step in analyzing this guilt feeling will be to discover that he really feels afraid of being found out and criticized by his parents, by his wife, by public opinion, by the church—briefly, by anyone who represents authority to him. Only then will he be able to recognize that behind this authoritarian feeling of guilt is another feeling. He will recognize that his "love" affairs are in reality expressions of his fear of love, of his inability to love anyone, to commit himself to any close and responsible relationship. He will recognize that his sin is against himself, the sin of letting his power to love go to waste.

Many other patients are not bothered with a sense of guilt at all. They complain about psychogenetic symptoms, depressed moods, inability to work or lack of happiness in their married life. But here too the analytic process uncovers a hidden sense of guilt. The patient learns to understand that neurotic symptoms are not isolated phenomena which can be dealt with independently from moral problems. He will become aware of his own conscience and begin to listen to its voice.

The function of the analyst is to help him in this

awareness, but not as an authority, a judge who has the right to summon the patient to account. He speaks as a person called upon to be concerned with the patient's problems and with only the authority which his concern with the patient and with his own conscience gives him.

Once the patient has overcome his authoritarian reactions to guilt or his total neglect of the moral problem, we observe a new reaction which is very much like the one I described as characteristic of humanistic religious experience. The role of the analyst in this process is a very restricted one. He can ask questions which make it more difficult for the patient to defend his loneliness by taking refuge in self-pity or by any of the many avenues of escape. He can be encouraging, as the presence of any sympathetic human being is to one who feels frightened, and he can help the patient by clarifying certain connections and by translating the symbolic language of dreams into the language of our waking life. But there is nothing the analyst, or any other person for that matter, can do to replace the patient's laborious process of sensing, feeling, and experiencing what goes on in his own soul. Indeed, this kind of soul searching does not require the analyst. Anyone can do it if he has some confidence in his own powers and if he is willing to bear some pain. Most of us succeed in waking up at a certain time in the morning if we have made up our minds firmly before going to sleep that we want to wake up at that time. To wake ourselves up in the sense of opening our eyes to what has been obscured is more difficult but it can be done provided we seriously want it. One thing must be made clear. There are no prescriptions which can be found in a few books about right living or the way to happiness. Learning to listen to one's conscience and to react to it does not lead to any smug and lulling "peace of mind" or "peace of soul." It leads to peace *with* one's conscience—not a passive state of bliss and satisfaction but continuous sensitivity to our conscience and the readiness to respond to it.

I have tried to show in this chapter that the psychoanalytic cure of the soul aims at helping the patient to achieve an attitude which can be called religious in the humanistic though not in the authoritarian sense of the word. It seeks to enable him to gain the faculty to see the truth, to love, to become free and responsible, and to be sensitive to the voice of his conscience. But am I not, the reader may ask, describing here an attitude which is more rightly called ethical than religious? Am I not leaving out the very element which distinguishes the religious from the ethical realm? I believe that the difference between the religious and the ethical is to a large extent only an epistemological one, though not entirely so. Indeed, it seems that there is a factor common to certain kinds of religious experience which goes beyond the purely ethical.[9] But

9. The kind of religious experience which I have in mind in these remarks is the one characteristic of Indian religious experience, Christian and Jewish mysticism, and Spinoza's pantheism. I should like to note that, quite in contrast to a popular sentiment that mysticism is an irrational type of religious experience, it represents—like Hindu and Buddhistic thought and Spinozism—the

it is exceedingly difficult if not impossible to formu-
late this factor of religious experience. Only those
who experience it will understand the formulation,
and they do not need any formulation. This difficulty
is greater but not different in kind from that of expressing any feeling experience in word symbols,
and I want to make at least an attempt to indicate
what I mean by this specifically religious experience
and what its relation is to the psychoanalytic process.

One aspect of religious experience is the wondering, the marveling, the becoming aware of life and
of one's own existence, and of the puzzling problem of
one's relatedness to the world. Existence, one's own
existence and that of one's fellow men, is not taken for
granted but is felt as a problem, is not an answer but
a question. Socrates' statement that wonder is the
beginning of all wisdom is true not only for wisdom
but for the religious experience. One who has never
been bewildered, who has never looked upon life and
his own existence as phenomena which require answers
and yet, paradoxically, for which the only answers
are new questions, can hardly understand what religious experience is.

Another quality of religious experience is what
Paul Tillich has called the "ultimate concern." It is
not passionate concern with the fulfillment of our desires but the concern connected with the attitude of
wonder I have been discussing: an ultimate concern

---

highest development of rationality in religious thinking. As Albert
Schweitzer has put it: "Rational thinking which is free from as-
sumptions ends in mysticism." *Philosophy of Civilization* (Macmil-
lan Company, 1949), p. 79.

with the meaning of life, with the self-realization of man, with the fulfillment of the task which life sets us. This ultimate concern gives all desires and aims, inasmuch as they do not contribute to the welfare of the soul and the realization of the self, a secondary importance; in fact they are made unimportant by comparison with the object of this ultimate concern. It necessarily excludes division between the holy and the secular because the secular is subordinated to and molded by it.

Beyond the attitude of wonder and of concern there is a third element in religious experience, the one which is most clearly exhibited and described by the mystics. It is an attitude of oneness not only in oneself, not only with one's fellow men, but with all life and, beyond that, with the universe. Some may think that this attitude is one in which the uniqueness and individuality of the self are denied and the experience of self weakened. That this is not so constitutes the paradoxical nature of this attitude. It comprises both the sharp and even painful awareness of one's self as a separate and unique entity and the longing to break through the confines of this individual organization and to be one with the All. The religious attitude in this sense is simultaneously the fullest experience of individuality and of its opposite; it is not so much a blending of the two as a polarity from whose tension religious experience springs. It is an attitude of pride and integrity and at the same time of a humility which stems from experiencing oneself as but a thread in the texture of the universe.

Has the psychoanalytic process any bearing on this kind of religious experience?

That it presupposes an attitude of ultimate concern I have already indicated. It is no less true that it tends to awaken the patient's sense of wondering and questioning. Once this sense is awakened the patient will find answers which are his own. If it is not awakened, no answer the psychoanalyst can give, not even the best and truest one, will be of any use. This wondering is the most significant therapeutic factor in analysis. The patient has taken his reactions, his desires and anxieties for granted, has interpreted his troubles as the result of the actions of others, of bad luck, constitution, or what not. If the psychoanalysis is effective it is not because the patient accepts new theories about the reasons of his unhappiness but because he acquires a capacity for being genuinely bewildered; he marvels at the discovery of a part of himself whose existence he had never suspected.

It is this process of breaking through the confines of one's organized self—the ego—and of getting in touch with the excluded and disassociated part of oneself, the unconscious, which is closely related to the religious experience of breaking down individuation and feeling one with the All. The concept of the unconscious however, as I use it here, is neither quite that of Freud nor that of Jung.

In Freud's thinking the unconscious is essentially that in us which is bad, the repressed, that which is incompatible with the demands of our culture and of our higher self. In Jung's system the unconscious becomes a source of revelation, a symbol for that which in religious language is God himself. In his view the fact that we are subject to the dictates of our unconscious is in itself a religious phenomenon. I believe that both these concepts of the unconscious are one-sided distortions of the truth. Our unconscious— that is, that part of our self which is excluded from the organized ego which we identify with our self— contains both the lowest and the highest, the worst and the best. We must approach the unconscious not as if it were a God whom we must worship or a dragon we must slay but in humility, with a profound sense of humor, in which we see that other part of ourselves as it is, neither with horror nor with awe. We discover in ourselves desires, fears, ideas, insights which have been excluded from our conscious organization and we have seen in others but not in ourselves. It is true, by necessity we can realize only a limited part of all the potentialities within us. We have to exclude many others, since we could not live our short and limited life without such exclusion. But outside the confines of the particular organization of ego are all human potentialities, in fact, the whole of humanity. When we get in touch with this disassociated part we retain the individuation of our ego structure but we experience this unique and individualized ego as only one of the infinite versions of life, just as a drop from the ocean is different from and yet the same as all other drops which are also only particularized modes of the same ocean.

In getting in touch with this disassociated world of the unconscious one replaces the principle of repression by that of permeation and integration. Repression is an act of force, of cutting off, of "law and order." It destroys the connection between our ego and the unorganized life from which it springs and makes our self into something finished, no longer growing but dead. In dissolving repression we permit ourselves to sense the living process and to have faith in life rather than in order.

I cannot leave the discussion of the religious function of psychoanalysis—incomplete as it is—without mentioning briefly one more factor of great significance. I am referring to something which has frequently been one of the greatest objections to Freud's method, the fact that so much time and effort is devoted to a single person. I believe that there is perhaps no greater evidence of Freud's genius than his counsel to take the time even if it should require many years to help one person to achieve freedom and happiness. This idea is rooted in the spirit of the Enlightenment which, crowning the whole humanistic trend of Western civilization, emphasized the dignity and uniqueness of the individual beyond everything else. But closely as it is in accord with these principles, such an idea is in contrast to much in the intellectual climate of our time. We tend to think in terms of mass production and of gadgets. As far as production of commodities is concerned this has proven exceedingly fruitful. But if the idea of mass production and gadget worship is transferred to the problem of man and into the field of psychiatry it destroys the very basis which makes producing more and better things worth while.

IS PSYCHOANALYSIS A THREAT
TO RELIGION?

I HAVE tried to show so far that only if we differentiate between authoritarian and humanistic
religion and between "adjustment counseling" and
"cure of the soul" can we try to answer this question.
But so far I have neglected to discuss various aspects
of religion which must be differentiated from each
other in order to determine which are threatened by
psychoanalysis and other factors in modern culture
and which are not. The particular aspects I wish to
discuss from this standpoint are the experiential aspect, the scientific-magical aspect, the ritualistic
aspect, the semantic aspect.

By experiential aspect I mean religious feeling and
devotion. The attitude common to the teachings of
the founders of all great Eastern and Western religions is one in which the supreme aim of living
is a concern with man's soul and the unfolding of
his powers of love and reason. Psychoanalysis, far
from being a threat to this aim, can on the contrary
contribute a great deal to its realization. Nor can
this aspect be threatened by any other science. It is
not conceivable that any discovery made by the natural sciences could become a threat to religious feeling.
On the contrary, an increased awareness of the nature
of the universe in which we live can only help man to

become more self-reliant and more humble. As for the social sciences, their growing understanding of man's nature and of the laws governing his existence contributes to the development of a religious attitude rather than threatens it.

The threat to the religious attitude lies not in science but in the predominant practices of daily life. Here man has ceased to seek in himself the supreme purpose of living and has made himself an instrument serving the economic machine his own hands have built. He is concerned with efficiency and success rather than with his happiness and the growth of his soul. More specifically the orientation which most endangers the religious attitude is what I have called the "marketing orientation" of modern man.[1]

The marketing orientation has established its dominant role as a character pattern only in the modern era. In the personality market all professions, occupations, and statuses appear. Employer, employee, and free-lance—each must depend for material success on personal acceptance by those who would use his services.

Here, as in the commodity market, *use* value is not sufficient to determine *exchange* value. The "personality factor" takes precedence over skills in the assessment of market value and most frequently plays the deciding role. While it is true that the most winning personality cannot make up for a total lack of skill— indeed, our economic system could not function on

1. Cf. the chapter on the marketing orientation in *Man for Himself*.

such a basis—it is seldom that skill and integrity alone account for success. Success formulae are expressed in such terms as "selling oneself," "getting one's personality across," and "soundness," "ambition," "cheerfulness," "aggressiveness," and so forth, which are stamped on the prize-winning personality package. Such other intangibles as family background, clubs, connections, and influence are also important desiderata and will be advertised however subtly as basic ingredients of the commodity offered. To belong to a religion and to practice it is also widely regarded as one of the requirements for success. Every profession, every field has its successful personality type. The salesman, the banker, the foreman, and the headwaiter have met the requirements, each in a different way and to a different degree, but their roles are identifiable, they have measured up to the essential condition: to be in demand.

Inevitably man's attitude toward himself is conditioned by these standards for success. His feeling of self-esteem is not based primarily on the value of his powers and the use he makes of them in a given society. It depends on his salability on the market, or the opinion others have about his "attractiveness." He experiences himself as a commodity designed to attract on the most favorable, the most expensive terms. The higher the offered price the greater the affirmation of his value. Commodity man hopefully displays his label, tries to stand out from the assortment on the counter and to be worthy of the highest price tag, but if he is passed by while others are snapped up he is convicted of inferiority and worthlessness. However high he may be rated in terms of both human qualities and utility, he may have the ill-luck—and must bear the blame—of being out of fashion.

From early childhood he has learned that to be in fashion is to be in demand and that he too must adapt to the personality mart. But the virtues he is taught—ambition, sensitivity, and adaptibility to the demands of others—are qualities too general to provide the patterns for success. He turns to popular fiction, the newspapers, and the movies for more specific pictures of the success story and finds the smartest, the newest models on the market to emulate.

It is hardly surprising that under these circumstances man's sense of his value must suffer severely. The conditions for his self-esteem are beyond his control. He is dependent on others for approval and in constant need of it; helplessness and insecurity are the inevitable results. Man loses his own identity in the marketing orientation; he becomes alienated from himself.

If man's highest value is success, if love, truth, justice, tenderness, mercy are of no use to him, he may *profess* these ideals but he does not *strive* for them. He may think that he worships the god of love but he actually worships an idol which is the idealization of his real goals, those rooted in the marketing orientation. Those who are concerned only with survival of religion and of the churches may accept the situation. Man will seek the haven of the church and of religion because his inner emptiness impels him to seek for some shelter. But professing religion does not mean being religious.

Those, however, who are concerned with religious experience, whether they are religionists or not, will not delight in seeing the churches crowded and in conversions. They will be the most severe critics of our secular practices and recognize that man's alienation from himself, his indifference to himself and to others, which have their roots in our whole secular culture are the real threats to a religious attitude, not psychology or any other science.

Quite different however is the impact of scientific progress on another aspect of religion, its *scientific-magical* one.

In his early attempts to survive man was hampered both by his lack of understanding of the forces of nature and by his relative helplessness to use them. He formulated theories about nature and devised certain practices for coping with it which became part of his religion. I call this aspect of religion a scientific-magical one because it shared with science the function of understanding nature in order to develop techniques for its successful manipulation. As long as man's knowledge of nature and his ability to control it were little developed this aspect of religion was necessarily a very important segment of his thinking. If he wondered about the movement of the stars, the growth of trees, how floods, lightning, and earthquakes came about, he could devise hypotheses which explained these occurrences in analogy with his human experience. He assumed that gods and demons were behind such events just as he recognized in the occurrences in his own life the arbitrary controls and influences of human relationships. When the productive forces man was to create in agriculture and in the manufacture of commodities were undeveloped he had to pray to his gods for help. If he needed rain he prayed for it. If he needed better crops he prayed to the goddesses of fertility. If he feared floods and earthquakes he prayed to the gods he thought responsible for these occurrences. In fact, it is possible to infer from the history of religion the level of science and technical development reached in various historical periods. Man turned to the gods to satisfy those practical needs which he himself could not properly provide for; those needs for which he did not pray were already within his power to satisfy. The more man understands and masters nature the less he needs to use religion as a scientific explanation and as a magical device for controlling nature. If mankind is able to produce enough to feed all men, it does not need to pray for daily bread. Man can provide that by his own efforts. The further scientific and technical progress is advanced the less need there is to charge religion with a task which is religious only in historical terms, not in terms of religious experience. Western religion has made this scientific–magical aspect an intrinsic part of its system and thus has put itself in opposition to the progressive development of human knowledge. This is not true of the great religions of the East. They have always had a tendency to differentiate sharply between that part of religion which deals with

man and those aspects which attempt an explanation
of nature. Questions which have given rise to violent
arguments and persecutions in the West, such as
whether the world is finite or not, whether or not the
universe is eternal, and others of the same type,
have been treated by Hinduism and Buddhism with
fine humor and irony. Buddha when questioned by
his pupils on such matters answered again and again:
"I do not know and it is of no concern to me because
whatever the answer is it does not contribute to the
one problem which is of concern: how to reduce human suffering." The same spirit is beautifully expressed in one of the Rigvedas:

"Who verily knows and who can here declare it,
    whence it was born and whence comes this creation?
The Gods are later than this world's production.
    Who knows then whence it first came into being?
He, the first origin of this creation, whether he
    formed it all or did not form it,
Whose eye controls this world in highest heaven, he
    verily knows it, *or perhaps he knows not.*" [2]

With the tremendous development of scientific
thinking and the progress in industry and agriculture
the conflict between the scientific statements of religion and those of modern science inevitably became
more and more acute. Most of the antireligious arguments of the Enlightenment period were directed not
against the religious attitude but against the claim of
religion that its scientific statements had to be taken

2. *The Hymns of the Rigveda*, Ralph T. H. Griffith, trans. (E. J.
Lazarus & Company, 1897), II, 576.

on faith. In recent years many attempts have been made both by religionists and by a number of scientists to show that the conflict between religious views and views suggested by the most recent developments in the natural sciences is diminished from what it was supposed to be even fifty years ago. A vast amount of data has been presented to lend support to this thesis. But I believe these arguments miss the central issue. Even if one were to say that the Judaeo-Christian view of the origin of the world is as tenable a scientific hypothesis as any other, the argument deals with the scientific aspect of religion and not with the religious one. The answer that what matters is the welfare of man's soul and that hypotheses about nature and its creation are of no relevance to this problem is still as true as it was when the Vedas or Buddha stated it.

In our discussion in the previous chapters I have neglected the *ritualistic* aspect of religion, although rituals are among the most important elements in every religion. Psychoanalysts have given special attention to ritual because their observations of patients seemed to promise new insights into the nature of its religious forms. They have found that certain types of patients perform rituals of a private nature which have nothing to do with their religious thinking or practice and yet seem to resemble the religious forms very closely. Psychoanalytic investigation can show that compulsive, ritualistic behavior is the outcome of intense affects which in themselves are not evident to the patient and with which he copes behind his own back, as it were, in the form of the ritual. In a particular case of washing compulsion one discovers that the washing ritual is an attempt to get rid of a strong sense of guilt. This sense of guilt is not caused by anything the patient has actually done but by destructive impulses which he is not conscious of. In the washing ritual he constantly undoes the destruction which he unconsciously has planned and which must never reach his consciousness. He needs this washing ritual in order to cope with his feeling of guilt. Once he is aware of the existence of the destructive impulse he can deal with it directly and by understanding the source of his destructiveness can eventually reduce it to an at least tolerable degree. The compulsive ritual has an ambiguous function. It protects the patient from an unbearable feeling of guilt but it also tends to perpetuate those impulses because it deals with them only indirectly.

No wonder that those psychoanalysts who turned their attention to religious rituals were struck by the similarity of the private compulsive rituals they observed in their patients to the socially patterned ceremonies they found in religion. They expected to find that the religious rituals followed the same mechanism as the neurotic compulsions. They looked for the unconscious drives, as, for instance, destructive hate of the father figure represented by God, which they felt must be either directly expressed or warded off in the ritual. Undoubtedly psychoanalysts in pursuing this course have made an important discovery about the nature of many religious rituals even though they may not always have been right in their specific explanations. But being preoccupied with pathological phenomena they often failed to see that rituals are not necessarily of the irrational nature found in the neurotic compulsion. They did not differentiate between these irrational rituals based upon repression of irrational impulses and the *rational rituals* which are of an entirely different nature.

We not only have the need for a frame of orientation which makes some sense of our existence and which we can share with our fellow men; we also have the need to express our devotion to dominant values by *actions* shared with others. A ritual, broadly speaking, is *shared action expressive of common strivings rooted in common values.*

The rational differs from the irrational ritual primarily in its function; it does not *ward off* repressed impulses but *expresses* strivings which are recognized as valuable by the individual. Consequently it does not have the obsessional-compulsive quality so characteristic of the irrational ritual; if the latter even once is not performed, the repressed threatens to break in, and therefore any lapse is accompanied by considerable anxiety. No such consequences are attached to any lapse in the performance of the rational ritual; nonperformance may be regretted but it is not feared. In fact, one can always recognize the irrational ritual by the degree of fear produced by its violation in any manner.

Simple examples of contemporary secular rational rituals are our habits of greeting another person, of honoring an artist by applauding, of showing reverence to the dead; [3] and many others.

Religious rituals are by no means always irrational. (To the observer who does not understand their meaning they of course always appear to be irrational.) A religious ritual of washing can be understood as a meaningful and rational expression of an inner cleansing without any obsessional or irrational component, as a symbolic expression of our wish for inner purity performed as ritual to prepare for an activity requiring full concentration and devotion. In the same way, rituals such as fasting, religious marriage ceremonies, concentration and meditation practices can be entirely rational rituals, in need of no analysis except for the one which leads to an understanding of their intended meaning.

Just as the symbolic language which we find in dreams and in myths is a particular form of expressing thoughts and feelings by images of sensory experience, the ritual is a symbolic expression of thoughts and feelings by *action*.

The contribution which psychoanalysis can make toward the understanding of rituals is in showing the psychological roots for the need of ritualistic action and in differentiating those rituals which are compul-

3. These simple rituals are not necessarily as rational as this discussion would make it appear. In rituals relating to death, for instance, there can be a greater or lesser component of repressed irrational elements motivating the ritual, for instance, overcompensation for repressed hostility against a dead person, reaction against intense fear of death, and magical attempts to protect oneself from this danger.

sive and irrational from those which are expressions of common devotion to our ideals.

What is the situation today as far as the ritualistic aspect of religions is concerned? The practicing religionist participates in the various rituals of his church and undoubtedly this very feature is one of the most significant reasons for church attendance. Because there is little opportunity for modern man to share actions of devotion with others, any form of ritual has a tremendous attraction even if it is cut off from the most significant feelings and strivings of one's everyday life.

The need for common rituals is thoroughly appreciated by the leaders of authoritarian political systems. They offer new forms of politically colored ceremonies which satisfy this need and bind the average citizen to the new political creed by means of it. Modern man in democratic cultures does not have many meaningful rituals. It is not surprising then that the need for ritualistic practice has taken all sorts of diversified forms. Elaborate rituals in lodges, rituals in connection with patriotic reverence for the state, rituals concerned with polite behavior, and many others are expressions of this need for shared action, yet often they exhibit only the impoverishment of devotional aim and separation from those ideals officially recognized by religion and ethics. The appeal of fraternal organizations, like the preoccupation with proper behavior expressed in etiquette books, gives convincing proof of modern man's need for ritual and of the emptiness of those he performs.

The need for ritual is undeniable and vastly under-estimated. It would seem that we are left with the alternatives of becoming religionists or indulging in meaningless ritualistic practices or living without any gratification of this need. If rituals could be easily devised new humanistic ones might be created. Such an attempt was made by the spokesmen for the religion of Reason in the eighteenth century. It has been made by the Quakers in their rational humanistic rituals and has been tried by small humanistic congregations. But rituals cannot be manufactured. They depend on the existence of genuinely shared common values, and only to the extent to which such values emerge and become part of human reality can we expect the emergence of meaningful, rational rituals.

In discussing the meaning of rituals we have already touched upon the fourth aspect of religion, the *semantic* one. Religion in its teachings as well as in its rituals speaks in a language different from the one we use in daily life, that is, in symbolic language. The essence of symbolic language is that inner experiences, ones of thought and feeling, are expressed as if they were sensory experiences. All of us "speak" this language if only when we are asleep. Yet the language of dreams is not different from that which is employed in myths and religious thinking. Symbolic language is the only universal language the human race has known. It is the language used in myths five thousand years old and in the dreams of our contemporaries. It is the same language in India and

China and in New York and Paris.[4] In societies where the primary concern was with understanding inner experiences this language was not only spoken but also understood. In our culture, though it is still spoken in dreams it is rarely understood. This misunderstanding consists mainly in taking the contents of symbolic language for real events in the realm of things instead of for symbolic expression of the soul's experience. On the basis of this misunderstanding dreams were considered to be nonsensical productions of our imagination and religious myths were thought to be childish concepts of reality.

It was Freud who made this forgotten language accessible to us. By his efforts to understand the language of dreams he has opened the road to an understanding of the peculiarities of symbolic language and has shown its structure and meaning. Simultaneously he has demonstrated that the language of religious myths is essentially not different from that of dreams, that it is a meaningful expression of significant experiences. While it is true that his interpretation of dreams and myths is narrowed by his overemphasis on the significance of the sexual drive, he has nevertheless laid the foundations for a new understanding of religious symbols in myth, dogma, and ritual. This comprehension of the language of symbols does not lead to a return to religion

4. The truth of this statement has been beautifully demonstrated by Joseph Campbell in his remarkable book, *The Hero with a Thousand Faces* (Bollingen Foundation, Inc., 1949).

but it does lead to a new appreciation of the profound and significant wisdom expressed by religion in symbolic language.

The foregoing considerations show that the answer to what constitutes the threat to religion today depends on what specific aspect of religion we are referring to. The underlying theme of the preceding chapters is the conviction that the problem of religion is not the problem of God but the problem of man; religious formulations and religious symbols are attempts to give expression to certain kinds of human experience. What matters is the nature of these experiences. The symbol system is only the cue from which we can infer the underlying human reality. Unfortunately the discussion centered around religion since the days of the Enlightenment has been largely concerned with the affirmation or negation of a belief in God rather than with the affirmation or negation of certain human attitudes. "Do you believe in the existence of God?" has been made the crucial question of religionists and the denial of God has been the position chosen by those fighting the church. It is easy to see that many who profess the belief in God are in their human attitude idol worshipers or men without faith, while some of the most ardent "atheists," devoting their lives to the betterment of mankind, to deeds of brotherliness and love, have exhibited faith and a profoundly religious attitude. Centering the religious discussion on the acceptance or denial of the symbol God blocks the understanding of the religious problem as a human problem and prevents the development of that human attitude which can be called religious in a humanistic sense.

Many attempts have been made to retain the symbol God but to give it a meaning different from the one which it has in the monotheistic tradition. One of the outstanding illustrations is Spinoza's theology. Using strictly theological language he gives a definition of God which amounts to saying there is no God in the sense of the Judaeo-Christian tradition. He was still so close to the spiritual atmosphere in which the symbol God seemed indispensable that he was not aware of the fact that he was negating the existence of God in the terms of his new definition.

In the writings of a number of theologians and philosophers in the nineteenth century and at present one can detect similar attempts to retain the word God but to give it a meaning fundamentally different from that which it had for the Prophets of the Bible or for the Christian and Jewish theologians of the Middle Ages. There need be no quarrel with those who retain the symbol God although it is questionable whether it is not a forced attempt to retain a symbol whose significance is essentially historical. However this may be, one thing is certain. The real conflict is not between belief in God and "atheism" but between a humanistic, religious attitude and an attitude which is equivalent to idolatry regardless of how this attitude is expressed —or disguised—in conscious thought.

Even from a strictly monotheistic standpoint the use of the word God constitutes a problem. The

Bible insists that man must not attempt to make an image of God in any form. Undoubtedly one aspect of this injunction is that of a tabu, guarding the awesomeness of God. Another aspect however is the idea that God is a symbol of all that which is in man and yet which man is not, a symbol of a spiritual reality which we can strive to realize in ourselves and yet can never describe or define. God is like the horizon which sets the limitations of our sight. To the naïve mind it seems to be something real which can be grasped, yet to seek the horizon is to seek a mirage. When we move, the horizon moves. When we climb even a low hill the horizon becomes wider, but it still remains a limitation and never is a *thing* to be taken hold of. The idea that God cannot be defined is clearly expressed in the biblical story of God's revelation to Moses. Moses, charged with the task of speaking to the children of Israel and leading them from bondage to freedom, yet knowing the spirit of serfdom and idolatry in which they lived, said to God: "Behold, when I come unto the children of Israel, and shall say unto them, The God of your fathers hath sent me unto you; and they shall say to me, What is his name? what shall I say unto them? And God said unto Moses, I AM THAT I AM: and he said, Thus shalt thou say unto the children of Israel, I AM hath sent me unto you." [5]

The meaning of these words becomes even clearer if we pay closer attention to the Hebrew text. "I am that I am" (*ehje asher ehje*) would be translated

5. Exodus 3:13-14.

more correctly in the tense used in the original: "I am being that I am being." Moses asks God for a name because a name is something one can grasp and worship. God throughout the whole story of Exodus has made loving concessions to the idola-trous state of mind of the children of Israel, and so he also makes the concession of telling Moses his name. But there is profound irony in this name. It expresses the process of being rather than something finite that could be named like a thing. The meaning of the text would be accurately rendered if it were trans-lated "My name is NAMELESS."

In the development of Christian and Jewish theol-ogy we find repeated attempts to achieve a purer concept of God by avoiding even a trace of positive description or definition of God (Plotinus, Maimon-ides). As the great German mystic, Master Eckhart, put it: "That which one says is God, he is not; that which one does not say of him he is more truly than that which one says he is." [6]

From the standpoint of monotheism carried through to its logical consequences there can be no argument about the nature of God; no man can pre-sume to have any knowledge of God which permits him to criticize or condemn his fellow men or to claim that his own idea of God is the only right one. The religious intolerance so characteristic of Western religions, which springs from such claims and, psy-chologically speaking, stems from lack of faith or lack of love, has had a devastating effect on religious

6. Fr. Pfeiffer, *Meister Eckhart* (1857).

development. It has led to a new form of idolatry. An image of God, not in wood and stone but in words, is erected so that people worship at this shrine. Isaiah has criticized this distortion of monotheism in these words:

"Wherefore have we fasted, say they, and thou seest not? wherefore have we afflicted our soul, and thou takest no knowledge? Behold, in the day of your fast ye find pleasure, and exact all your labours.

"Behold, ye fast for strife and debate, and to smite with the fist of wickedness: ye shall not fast as ye do this day, to make your voice to be heard on high.

"Is it such a fast that I have chosen? a day for a man to afflict his soul? is it to bow down his head as a bulrush, and to spread sackcloth and ashes under him? wilt thou call this a fast, and an acceptable day to the Lord?

"Is not this the fast that I have chosen? to loose the bands of wickedness, to undo the heavy burdens, and to let the oppressed go free, and that ye break every yoke?

"Is it not to deal thy bread to the hungry, and that thou bring the poor that are cast out to thy house? when thou seest the naked, that thou cover him; and that thou hide not thyself from thine own flesh?

"Then shall thy light break forth as the morning, and thine health shall spring forth speedily: and thy righteousness shall go before thee; the glory of the Lord shall be thy reward." [7]

The Old Testament, and particularly the Prophets,

7. Isaiah 58: 3–8.

are as much concerned with the negative, the fight against idolatry, as they are with the positive, the recognition of God. Are *we* still concerned with the problem of idolatry? Only when we find that certain "primitives" worship idols of wood and stone do we show such concern. We picture ourselves as being far above such worship and as having solved the problem of idolatry because we do not see ourselves worshiping any of these traditional symbols of idolatry. We forget that the essence of idolatry is not the worship of this or that particular idol but is a specifically human attitude. This attitude may be described as the deification of things, of partial aspects of the world and man's submission to such things, in contrast to an attitude in which his life is devoted to the realization of the highest principles of life, those of love and reason, to the aim of becoming what he potentially is, a being made in the likeness of God. It is not only pictures in stone and wood that are idols. Words can become idols, and machines can become idols; leaders, the state, power, and political groups may also serve. Science and the opinion of one's neighbors can become idols, and God has become an idol for many.

While it is not possible for man to make valid statements about the positive, about God, it is possible to make such statements about the negative, about idols. Is it not time to cease to argue about God and instead to unite in the unmasking of contemporary forms of idolatry? Today it is not Baal and Astarte but the deification of the state and of power in authoritarian countries and the deification of the machine and of success in our own culture which threaten the most precious spiritual possessions of man. Whether we are religionists or not, whether we believe in the necessity for a new religion or in a religion of no religion or in the continuation of the Judaeo-Christian tradition, inasmuch as we are concerned with the essence and not with the shell, with the experience and not with the word, with man and not with the church, we can unite in firm negation of idolatry and find perhaps more of a common faith in this negation than in any affirmative statements about God. Certainly we shall find more of humility and of brotherly love.